CONCILIUM

concilium

1990/3

ASKING AND THANKING

Edited by

Christian Duquoc and
Casiano Florestan

SCM Press · London
Trinity Press International · Philadelphia

June 1990

ISBN: 0 334 03002 1

Typeset at The Spartan Press Ltd, Lymington, Hants
Printed by Dotesios Printers Ltd, Trowbridge, Wilts

Concilium: Published February, April, June, August, October, December.

Contents

Editorial

So close is the relationshp between prayer and religion that any shift in the acceptance or rejection of the experience of prayer is always an important symptom of appreciation of or disinterest in the religious phenomenon. To put it another way, although prayer is the soul of religious experience, any criticism or defence of prayer is at the same time the rejection or acceptance of religion itself. Of course, just as religion has been understood and is understood in different ways, so prayer is offered and understood in thousands of ways, given that prayer fluctuates between commitment and evasion, an act of faith or magic, personal experience and empty ritualism. In fact in some highly secularized circles it costs a lot to say that one prays; by contrast, in groups with a coherent religious practice one can be ashamed to say that one does not pray. In either case, prayer does not leave us indifferent.

In this issue of *Concilium* we are not touching on the theme of prayer in general but on the question of the two basic types of prayer, namely petitionary prayer and prayer of thanksgiving. The first part begins with an anthropological study of prayer written by H. Schaller with the aim of illuminating the deep roots of asking and thanking. But prayer, both petitionary prayer and prayer of thanksgiving, is a universal phenomenon in the world of religions. Hence the examination of it by J. Martín Velasco. One particular and important instance of prayer, prior to Christian prayer, is the prayer of benediction, i.e. the rabbinic *berakhah*, which is studied by L. A. Hoffman. This legacy of Judaism was taken over and reformulated in depth by Jesus, whose petitionary prayers and thanksgivings are analysed exegetically by G. M. Soares-Prabhu. Up to this point the issue considers the legacy which Christianity received in connection with these two basic forms of prayer.

A second part of this issue is devoted to the real situation of prayer. It is obviously necessary to analyse contemporary criticisms of prayer in relation to the actual structure of prayer and the secular context in which it is offered today. The suspicions aroused by prayer are examined by

E. Bianchi. Basically, judgments on prayer are related to the pictures that we have of God. Prayer is the criterion of our talk about God. A theological analysis of prayer, in the two ways in which it is formulated, is made in the article by U. Eibach. Joan Llopis makes a survey of the prayer of the faithful and the eucharist with regard to its tradition, justification and importance, ending with a series of practical suggestions. The contribution by M. de Barros Souza is very concrete: it is concerned with popular Latin American Catholicism. This is the simple prayer of a poor and Christian people, formulated in the festive processions of the sanctuaries, which reflects a faith that is related to life. Isabelle Chareire has been asked to show how prayer, despite its orientation towards gratuitousness, is expressed through human beings who cannot hide their fragility, questions and desires.

The contributions contained in this issue of *Concilium* basically agree in formulating some criteria and some conclusions which can be summed up briefly as follows: 1. The basic nucleus of religious experience is prayer, to such a degree that there is no religion without prayer and no prayer without religion. Here prayer is understood as a personal relationship with the deity, the raising up of the soul to God, the awareness and welcoming of the presence of the mystery, respect for the human person and an absolute decision. 2. Of the innumerable forms of prayer, two stand out by virtue of their content: petitionary prayer and prayer of thanksgiving or praise. These two forms of prayer are not opposed but complementary; they are not exclusive but co-extensive. In making a petitionary prayer we are aware of our finitude and our sin, at the same time taking account of our responsibility and the struggle against evil and the task of transforming the world. When we offer thanks in the form of a prayer we recognize the God of life who pours out his love in abundance. These two forms of prayer correspond to two attitudes, namely of fear and fascination, of desire and of enjoyment, and also indicate that life understood in Christian terms is both hard work and grace. We need to remember that the terms 'pardon' (in asking) and 'thank you' (in recognition) are part of the basic vocabulary of any well-developed idiom and the framework of everyday life. 3. Prayer, and especially petitionary prayer, has been questioned in modern times from every possible perspective. It has been said that this type of prayer spoils our image of our God and our conception of human beings, while the prayer of thanksgiving presupposes a fictitious world which arises out of needs and desires. These criticisms of prayer are considered thoroughly in this issue and then given adequate answers. 4. Generally speaking, all the articles refer to the teaching of Jesus on prayer and the way in which he prayed, ending up with an examination of the reason why we should pray at all.

Prayer is not only a sign of being human: it is an act of faith and a reflection of the being of God. In the end, the Our Father is the model to which we refer petitionary prayer and thanksgiving; it is not a mere formula but a personal relationship and a direct religious experience. It is a recognition of human need and unworthiness, a confession of faith and an expression of trust in God.

Christian Duquoc
Casiano Floristan

Special Column 1990/3

The New Priests

While seminaries in Africa and Asia appear to be filling quite rapidly at the beginning of this decade, it would be illusory to think that this influx has changed the situation in which many communities have no resident priest, and as a result are frequently without a Sunday eucharist.[1] At the same time, in the northern hemisphere the beginning of the decade sees the continued decline in the number of priests, small entries into the seminaries, and an increasing number of parishes led by lay ministers, in the absence of a priest.

It is also often observed that in these northern countries at least, the closing decade was witness to the increased conservatism of newly ordained priests, with resultant problems for collaboration between faithful and ordained in the works of the ministry.[2]

One of the conclusions drawn from a series of sociological surveys in North America was that the shortage of candidates for ordination is a sign not of a spiritual but of an institutional crisis in the Roman Catholic Church.[3] By denying a spiritual crisis, it was meant that there is no lack of faith and devotion in the Catholic population, nor of an absence of readiness for ministry and service, as the number of persons engaged in lay ministries shows. The institutional crisis springs from the fact that the young men who would be viable candidates for the seminary according to present discipline are generally uninterested in accepting the conditions for ordination or life within the presbyterium. The role as presently conceived does not attract very many, even among those quite anxious to take on some form of ministry in the church. There is thus the irony that even while parishes lack ordained ministers, it is not very difficult to organize communities under lay leadership. This gives rise to an odd sacramental practice, just cause for preoccupation, but it also shows that the church is not wanting for persons who are ready for ministry and who are effective leaders. The profusion of ministries in churches on other continents, and the restructuring of communities to involve the faithful as a whole and to engage many types of ministry, has been frequently documented, even as the question of ordination remains on a whole unsettled.[4]

When in this critical situation one notes the conservatism of the more recently ordained, immune to any deep structural change, there is cause for concern. One has to ask how the maintenance of a conservative discipline in the choice and preparation of candidates for ordination affects the life of the Spirit in the church. It clearly has its repercussions on the flow of the Spirit and its charisms, and on the degree of participation asked of the baptized in the building up of the life of the church and of its mission. Obviously, it also promotes a special kind of priestly image and priestly spirituality, that has to be a matter for consideration at the forthcoming Synod of Bishops, called to consider the formation of priests in the circumstances of our day.

After the Second Vatican Council, there was considerable upheaval in the lives of priests, who found themselves functioning in pastoral situations quite diverse from those in which they had begun their ministry. Some felt unable to fit into the new patterns and sought release from ministry. Others, exposed to unwonted contacts with lay persons through changes in parish and rectory life, felt that celibacy was not as vital to priesthood as they had thought, or that at least it was not something that they could personally sustain. Among those who continued in their work, and among those ordained in the years after the Council, there was considerable enthusiasm for a newly structured church and mission. Despite opposition, hesitations and obstacles, there was a readiness to adopt innovative measures in promoting Christian life and the spread of the gospel. With this enthusiasm, there went the persuasion that new disciplines were needed in order to promote fuller participation in church life and in church ministry. Whether or not this was acknowledged, this implied a new outlook on the choice and preparation of candidates for ordination.

While authorities in the church repeatedly raise the question of what is needed in the preparation of priests who are able to respond to the issues of the day, by and large they have kept a conservative discipline with regard to ordination and promote a conservative image of the priestly role. Even while much more is asked of priests by way of work with the laity, there is a repeated emphasis on the distinction between priest and baptized which goes in the opposite direction and fosters spiritual and psychological tensions in the lives of priests.[5] Much of this emphasis is rightly intended to keep the laity from being clericalized in their ministerial roles, so that they keep open a sense of presence to the world. It is also, however, linked to an ideal of priesthood that is expressed in terms of a very distinctive relation to Jesus Christ and to the holy. This risks undermining church communion in favour of hierarchy.

In any case, the support-structures of priestly life and ministry, whether in the seminary or in the promotion of the diocesan presbyterium, are those which uphold a conservative order of ministry and of priestly identity, as well as a conservative attitude to the place of the religious and the holy in human society. It is the resistance to structural change, and to new types of relation between baptized and ordained, that is the hallmark of the kind of conservatism here intended. This is upheld by a type of theology that seems to look back to the Tridentine model of priesthood, even when the teaching of the Second Vatican Council is invoked. In an age when a measure of religious fundamentalism seems to be a common response to cultural change, it is not surprising that the candidates attracted to priesthood under such conditions, even while few, often exhibit a more conservative mentality.

Some have made a contrast between candidates within diocesan seminaries and those within religious communities, which may be enlightening, as it shows the role played by support systems. Those ordained in religious communities, it is said, are more likely to be innovative in their ministry, and in welcoming the ministry of the non-ordained.[6] This is attributed to the nature of the communities themselves. In their internal life, they do not lay great stress on the distinction between lay members and ordained members. They also have structures of government which are by nature participatory, promoting sharing, and supportive of new ventures in ministry. This cannot be taken as a general description of conditions in religious orders and congregations, but a point is made about what helps to promote new kinds of ministry that is worth considering.

The flow of candidates into seminaries in parts of Africa and Asia has already been noted. Since these continents are not prone to doing sociological surveys, there is less data on which to base observations about candidates. Attraction to priesthood, however, seems to be linked with two things that complement one another, in a way not easily comprehensible to other cultures. On the one hand, there is the foundation of a religious spirit, with its appeal to the holy, that still pervades the cultures of people in a way not now known in the northern hemisphere. On the other hand, some of the candidates come from communities with vibrant lay participation, and indeed have at times been themselves lay ministers and leaders in their local churches. To the extent that this happens, one can say that greater lay participation has actually served to promote the call to ordination. How in the years to come the religious spirit of these cultures is incorporated into the church, and how ministerial structures within communities develop, will clearly be vital to the future of ministry and priesthood. It would be unfortunate if candidates for ordination, on entering seminaries, were cut off from the base and given a motivation at odds with what is going on there. When pastors and people call for a change in the Tridentine model of priesthood, they are not simply thinking of the increase in the number of candidates that could be drawn outside the ranks of the seminary-trained and the celibate. They are more deeply concerned with the conditions necessary for the proper promotion of local churches, with their requirement for a different sort of leadership and liturgy.[7]

On the whole, in face of ministerial needs, one has the impression that the church has not persevered very well since the Second Vatican Council in the reading of the signs of the times. This has hindered it from learning from experience, and from relating the ordering of its life to this experience. Spiritualities and role imagery are conservative to the degree that they prevent experience from raising questions. It is the action of the Spirit in so many new ways that raises questions for the ordering of the church. It offers new insights into the call of God and into new models for common life and ministry that contrast with the old. Since the new experience is different on different continents, it exacts greater pluralism. Everywhere the fruits of the Spirit are there to be harvested. It is often the apparently innovative that is the most faithful to tradition, in a broader and fuller sense. Tradition, of its nature, requires openness to the new ways of the Spirit and a discernment of its action. While one cannot expect a hurried change in church ordering, it also has to be said that there is a certain urgency inherent to the times. If spiritual renewal, a strong sense of mission, and a new approach to church ordering do not go hand in hand, in the face of vast and rapid social and cultural change, those entering seminaries may well remain few in number and unfortunately ill-suited to the leadership that churches need.

Notes

1. For a recent overview of the situation across continents, cf. *Pro Mundi Vita Studies*, 12 November 1989. Note the remark in the concluding essay by Ernest Michel, 'Questions and Perspectives', p. 45: 'There is a need to overcome the still all too frequent gulf between the clergy, the possessors of authority and initiative, and the laity who are called to obey. Likewise we must overcome the clear-cut distinction between the laity whose job it is to transform the world, and the clergy, who are responsible for the internal life of the communities. This division of perspectives is not entirely satisfactory.'

2. Cf. Richard McBrien, 'Commentary', in Dean R. Hoge et al., *Research on Men's Vocations to the Priesthood and Religious Life*, United States Catholic Conference: Washington DC 1984, 77.

3. Cf. Dean R. Hoge, *The Future of Catholic Leadership. Responses to the Priest Shortage*, Kansas City, MO 1987, 215.

4. Two essays in *Pro Mundi Vita Studies*, no. 12, ask quite explicitly for a change from the Tridentine model of priest. Cf. Paul Rutayisire, 'Assemblies without the celebration of the Eucharist in Africa: a sign of hope or a sign of crisis in the ministry', 14. Mil Roekaerts, 'The Asian Scene in Parishes without a Resident Priest', 39–41, recounts the efforts of the Indonesian bishops to 'revise the Tridentine model of priests' in order to have truly local churches that are people-centred.

5. Chapter 2 of John Paul II, *Christifideles Laici*, is a strong call for a community-centred collaborative ministry, yet it continues to promote the Tridentine image of the priest.

6. Cf. Eugene Hemrick & Dean R. Hoge, *Seminarians in Theology. A National Profile*, Washington DC: USCC 1985.

7. As noted above, notes 1 and 4.

David N. Power OMI

Asking and Thanking – A Meaningful Unity

Hans Schaller

In our everyday life we make requests and on many occasions say 'Thank you'. In so doing we use words which are familiar to us and come naturally to our lips. They are part of our everyday behaviour, part of communication, and their meaningfulness is taken for granted.

I want to enquire into what we take for granted, in other words what we presuppose without questioning as we make requests and give thanks. What is bound up with a request or a word of thanks? What are the deeper dimensions of this everyday behaviour?

Asking as a mark of being human

There is a sentence of Seneca's which can help us to discover the anthropological significance of making requests. It runs: 'That which is given without asking is more precious and valuable than that which is given on request.' This statement is illuminating and plausible, and its correctness can be checked at many points of our everyday life. To give just a brief example: if we constantly have to remind a friend of our birthday, the friend is hardly showing signs of great affection; it would mean more to us, and be more in accord with the meaning of friendship, if the friend remembered automatically. There is something painful to both sides about gestures, presents, which we have to prompt or which we even have to ask for. It is embarrassing always to have to call attention to the neglect of elementary obligations of friendship.

To put it in more general terms, affection which is expressed spontaneously, favours done without asking and almost without a reason, are a more direct sign of love than attention which is begged for. They bear witness to a spontaneity of affection, a sympathy from the wellspring of being, the special value of a first step. Understood in these terms, Seneca's meaning is clear.

However, if we look closer, we note that though this statement is clear and verifiable, it remains one-sided. As a statement it covers only what makes an answer valuable, the value of the motives of our action. However, it does not cover the essence of the request, the specific nature of this act of communication. The nature of making requests becomes clearest where the content of the request is not a material but a spiritual need, where existential interests are also involved, for example in the request for time to listen, for forgiveness for a bad action, for consideration and patience. In such requests, which reveal personal grief and human dependence, it becomes clear what is happening between two people when a request is made. They are not using a means of requiring or even extracting something from each other but are bearing witness to a mutual trust. It is an exchange, a mutual challenge, a giving and taking.

The friend who, for example, ventures to ask a companion to spare some time is recognizing the need of someone who is close and will listen. He or she acknowledges need and dependence and takes the risk of opening up a little more. At the same time he or she counts on this confession being accepted, and not rejected or ridiculed. He or she hopes for a generous acceptance of a need, a friendly response to distress. That makes the formal structure of the request clear: it is based on the one hand on the acknowledgment of dependence, on a humble appreciation of the creaturely situation of men and women. On the other hand the request carries with it the hope that it will be fulfilled. 'Prayer calls for a perpetual need for hope, which is humble enough really to ask, and at the same time arrogant enough to expect that the request will be fulfilled' (Josef Pieper, *Hoffnung und Geschichte*, Munich 1967, 75).

Asking as a criterion of trust

With this thought we now touch on the real difficulty in Seneca's comment on the phenomenon of asking. What seems to him so precious about what is freely given is not so much the insight that spontaneity is of greater value, but the welcome situation that this avoids the need to ask. For such behaviour, in which dependence and vulnerability have to be conceded, is to be avoided. It is not seemly for human beings. Not to be adequate in spiritual or material respects contradicts the Stoic ideal and is therefore to be avoided wherever possible. According to Seneca, in prayer one as it were sinks below one's true level. In so doing one contradicts one's own worth, adopts the attitude of a slave or even of a cringing beggar; one makes oneself a pathetic figure, like the begging daughters of Zeus. They are 'lame of their feet, and wrinkled, and cast their eyes sidelong' (Homer, *Iliad*, 9,502).

Such negative evaluations of the attitude of asking have to be answered with counter-questions: what is more appropriate to human nature, the demonstration of self-sufficiency, an apparently autonomous capacity to look after oneself, or a humble recognition of need? Is not the request something very human, a quite special sign of trust, precisely because it calls for the recognition of one's own dependence and also expresses this directly or indirectly? Is it not the real criterion for the quality of prevailing trust, a kind of test by which the degree of mutual affection is measured? Is it not a very human form of communication?

These questions find a positive echo, and do so in fact for two main reasons.

1. The strength of a trust, whether between God and human beings or between human beings, is always measured by the amount of room which is made for personal weaknesses, imperfections and needs. It is a special demonstration of trust when we can express our existential needs to other people and to friends. We always do this in the hope (albeit also with some sorrow) that the other person will hold fast even when mistakes and weaknesses become evident. Trust grows in personal relationships where we become free from the pressure of always having to cut a strong, independent, almost impeccable figure. Where we ask, we venture in a concrete way not to suppress or to cover up such need and inner distress, but to recognize it. We concede it and in so doing also become a little more true, a little more human.

The second reason why asking is human behaviour relates to the fact that we are spiritual beings. It is not the case, as we might perhaps be inclined to assume, that we are compelled to ask only because of our bodily nature and the needs to which it gives rise, or that material need, mutual external dependence, brings us together. Human forms of asking are not a specific consequence of our bodily situation, but arise, rather, from the midst of our spiritual existence.

As beings who are capable of knowledge, freedom and communication we can recognize our own need, formulate it and communicate it to others. We evaluate and assess ourselves; we can see our own deficiencies and weaknesses, and compensate for them in various ways. Within our own spiritual depths we can recognize ourselves as being essentially inadequate, living in great need and with an elemental hunger for love and understanding. Spirit and need are not mutually exclusive. On the contrary, they are very closely connected and indeed accentuate each other. Henri de Lubac put this very well: 'The more spiritual a creature, the greater the need.'

For this reason expressions of humanity which are concerned with our own need, weakness and dependence are not unworthy of us. They are far removed from being a negative characteristic of our existence; they are not a sign of deficiency which should not be and of which we must be ashamed. As true statements about our existence, as it were as concessions, as a sign of our humanity, they are an opportunity to be human.

Asking as an expression of friendship

Let us go back to Seneca again. A brief glance at simple interpersonal behaviour, particularly as this is to be found in friendship, shows that Seneca's view that asking lies below the level of a being endowed with the spirit is inadequate. It takes place at the cost of suppression. Let us reflect once again on where and in what sense requests are made in our everyday experience. A housewife asks a neighbour to look after the children for an afternoon. We ask a friend whether he or she has time to discuss an important decision with us. In so doing are we not stating that asking is quite a different matter from thanking? We know from experience that we can thank someone for a favour without any particular circumstances, but we cannot ask for it unquestioningly. Often we hesitate, wondering what we may ask of whom. This uncertainty is fully justified. For it is quite evident that depending on what a request involves, it presupposes a special basis of trust of which we must become certain. It makes greater demands on us than thanking, and brings generosity and readiness to help more into the centre of the picture. It is, as I have already said, the criterion of a trust.

Or, to mention another less obvious experience: perhaps we have already experienced, without paying any direct attention to it, that a friendship has entered another, higher stage when for the first time we have ventured to ask a friend for something – something that concerned us personally: time together, help in considering a problem, perhaps even a few days' holiday together. In some circumstances we have discovered that mutual trust grows where we risk something. We venture a great step where we acknowledge and concede dependence and need. The spiral of mutual trust goes one stage higher in such a concession and the active request that goes with it.

We can consolidate this notion that asking is a motivating force within a relationship by considering the opposite situation. Do we not also experience that human relationships, even friendships, are crippled, peter out or even die where nothing more is required, no more wishes are expressed, no requests are made? In such a situation does not trust atrophy, with the result that an important medium is kept out of the relationship? Here the formulation of wishes, asking for what one needs, is a means of resisting the slow decay and the barren adaptation of a relationship. For only the friend who asks is allowed to draw attention in a healing way to the atrophy of a mutual relationship, to insist on questions, to put himself or herself 'urgently' in the centre of the other person's freedom. Only such a friend can dare to speak the whole truth to the other person, for even though the collapse in the relationship may cause pain, it does not present this truth in a casual or uninvolved way but holds it out like a cloak, in which the friend can take refuge. 'Friendship requires that we ask our friends to keep their promises, not to take back their gifts, not to go back on their invitations. And just as we have to make demands on our friends, we can expect that our friends will also make demands on us' (Andrew Greeley, *The Friendship Game*, New York 1971).

Petitionary prayer based in thanksgiving

As human behaviour, asking itself raises questions. It has presuppositions, and calls for a trust which forms the foundation and the ground on which asking can grow and becomes possible.

This connection also has a specific application to petitionary prayer in the theological sphere. The appeal to the freedom of God, the call for the involvement of this freedom in our situation of need, has its roots in a relationship which God has established prior to our prayer. Through God's initiative we are declared children of God and admitted to his presence. It is his will that we should not keep silent before him but that we should be allowed to say something to him, indeed make requests to him with great urgency.

We owe this capacity to want something from God to a prevenient grace. It is a right that is granted to us by God, a privilege which remains bound up with our faith. It is not simply a natural disposition or a capacity that we may take for granted. Because we are children of God, we may dare to say 'Our Father'.

So where we venture to turn to God with a request, we also always implicitly give thanks. We recognize the degree to which our prayers are undeserved, and therefore know that without claims or merit on our part we are accepted by God himself, and are filled with his Spirit in which alone we can call on God and ask God in an appropriate way; only in this Spirit does the most intimate word of prayer, 'Abba, Father', which Jesus spoke before us, take shape (Rom. 8).

Only in this inner link with thanksgiving is prayer as an expression of our faith theologically possible and psychologically meaningful. Before all the justification we are given for asking and complaining, we therefore know that we owe our existence to another, that without our deserving, without any intrinsic necessity, we are created and redeemed. Only where our prayer of petition and lament arises on the foundation of such thanksgiving does it become different from a human arrogance, the idea that in a presumptuous and arrogant way we can make God concerned with our petty human life. This is also far removed from a demeaning kind of begging, in which we men and women would be lowering ourselves as we came before God. It is neither presumption nor a failure to heed our creatureliness, but an expression of our worth.

To sum up: prayer in all its forms is and remains a twofold challenge. It calls for an existential concession and is a struggle with our own creatureliness, a recognition of our inadequacy. On the other hand it is a venture! In appealing to the freedom of the other we risk trust and stake hope. The more deeply we understand the interpersonal phenomenon of asking, the more clearly we understand what goes on between human beings when they ask one another for something, the more easily we will find the way to the theological sphere, to petitionary prayer. The more firmly the concepts are anchored in anthropology, the more securely they are anchored in theology (and preserved from being ideology).

Translated by John Bowden

Petitionary Prayer and Thanksgiving in the World Religions

Juan Martín Velasco

The precise object of this article is to show the presence in world religions of the two forms of prayer referred to in the title, their distinguishing features and similarities. To do this, first we must define the idea of prayer we have in mind when describing these two forms of it. Then we must clarify the relationship of prayer to the complex of elements making up this vast world that we call the fact or phenomenon of religion.

Prayer, a central element of religious life

Students of the phenomenon of religion have expressed this centrality of prayer in countless images. Prayer has been called religion's heart, breath, soul, hearth.[1] It is so important in religious life that it has been said that it is the chief indicator of whether religion exists, and when prayer disappears there are reasons for thinking that religion has disappeared too.

Many arguments can be adduced to support such statements. Few of the many forms and manifestations that make up religious life are as widespread in all religions as prayer. Most of the sacred texts collected in the various traditions are composed of prayer formulas. The experience of prayer is one of the characteristic features in the life of founders and reformers of religions. The starting point of their activity is some prayer experience, whether in the form of illumination as in the Buddha's case, or revelation, vocation and mission as in the case of Zarathustra, the prophets of Israel, Jesus of Nazareth and Muhammad. Prayer is the chief expression of the religious attitude, from which all other expressions arise. Freely translating St Thomas's definition *oratio est proprie religionis actus*, we can say that prayer is the act of religion which is religion in action, the actualization and putting into practice of religion.[2] Such a close relationship between religion and prayer and the central place prayer holds in religious life as a whole explain why prayer constitutes a sort of summing-up of the religious, so that the whole of each religious system is condensed and reflected in the formulas and gestures it uses for prayer.

From the countless forms of prayer to the praying attitude as the common root of all of them

But does it make sense to talk of just 'prayer'? Because we find in the history of religions and the religious life of every individual an almost countless number of extraordinarily different prayers, impossible to categorize adequately. The primary reason for this is that each religious system sets its own mark on its most immediate expression, which is prayer. So, before we attempt any description it is evident that the prayer of Buddhism and the prayer of Israel expressed in the Psalms are two different activities, rooted in different attitudes. The same goes for Hindu prayer expressed in the Upanishads and the Muslim reciting the Qur'an, the prayer of a culture without writing and of peoples belonging to the great cultures of antiquity. But as well as this, within each one of these systems, people pray in ways as various as silence and a detailed litany listing their smallest needs, a cry for help and a hymn of praise, prayer for forgiveness and confession of faith.[3]

Even though I realize that it is impossible to make a full list or adequate classification, I now set out some of the most frequent types of prayer to help us find their common root or roots.

First, who prays? It may be an individual or a community, a single person or a group, large or small. Prayer may be private or official, according to whether the formula comes from a single person or group's own creativity or is sanctioned by the religious authority of the community. Depending on the person praying, it may be silent, mental, vocal or with gestures, and each of these can also vary with the use of different words, bodily movements or mental acts. Thus vocal prayer may be expressed in whispers, cries, murmurs, stammering, nonsense words or songs; praying by gesture may be done sitting or standing, with small or large movements, prostration, bowing, lifting the eyes or hands to heaven, even gentle or frenetic dancing. There are also classifications which take into account the degree of perfection and the greater or lesser commitment of the person praying. Thus the Christian tradition distinguishes reading, meditation, contemplation or recollection, quiet and union.[4]

Probably the most useful classifications if we want to discover the common root of prayer are those referring to the whole style, the fundamental religious disposition that it expresses, and the one classifying its forms with regard to its content. Beginning with the latter, we find that prayer covers an enormous plurality of forms. It may be a greeting, an invocation, offering, vow, propitiation, petition, asking for forgiveness, lament, praise, thanksgiving, confession of faith, act of submission, confident dialogue or simple awareness and exercise of union.

We only have to look at particular examples of each of the above forms to see that all these divisions are relative. The truth is that each of these forms contains elements and features of the others, so that we can say that every form of prayer, when it is authentic, is 'symphonic'. It unites in an original form what is fundamental in all the others, arranging it around a predominant feeling or attitude, according to the prayer's particular situation, cultural circumstances and the general type of religious behaviour to which it belongs.[5] Hence there is no vocal prayer which does not also assume that the mind is aware and working; that there is some sort of body posture and a good dose of listening and silence. There is no true community prayer except when the members of the group are personally involved in it. And in most religions there is no personal prayer which does not involve much that is communal, because it uses traditional formulas belonging to the community and is ready to pray for the other members of the group.[6]

Official prayer requires the adaptation of the formula to the circumstances of the person or group using it, as spontaneous prayer is frequently fed by ideas and feelings that are part of the religious traditions of the group, crystallized in its sacred texts. The same may be observed in relation to the forms of prayer according to the content of its formulas. True prayer of petition expresses consciousness of need, an attitude of confidence, confession of faith, awareness of unworthiness, praise of God. Just as there is no prayer of praise which does not also express the desire for salvation, an awareness of the distance between God and the worshipper and some form of asking for help.

Is it possible to detect beneath this profusion of different forms a common root that justifies us in calling them all by one name? The obvious plurality and variety of prayer forms derive from the variety of languages, cultures, traditions, situations, states of mind belonging to the worshipper. But in all these manifestations can we distinguish a common attitude characterizing the person at prayer?

Attempts to answer this question are made by the numerous definitions of prayer worked out by the different religious traditions and in a modern way by the science of religions. These answers also differ according to the ideas of religion held by their authors and by the religious facts that they have taken as prototypical. Thus Heiler, after listing and describing a large number of prayer forms, concludes his study of 'the essence of prayer' by summing it up as 'the reverential and trustful consciousness of the living presence of God'.[7] He notes as the elements of the inner structure of prayer 'faith in a living personal God, faith in his real, immediate presence, and a realistic fellowship into which man enters with a God conceived as present'.[8]

Clearly this description of prayer corresponds perfectly to the forms of prayer in the traditions which he identifies as prophetic: Mazdaism, Judaism, Christianity and Islam. But clearly too, it can only be applied to the prayer of the traditions which he identifies as mystical, especially Buddhism and Vedic Hinduism, with quite a few adaptations.

Therefore it seems truer to the facts either to recognize that the notion of prayer is analogical[9] or to propose a less strict definition, while indicating the particular forms that it takes in the different religious traditions and actual prayers. In this sense I think the praying attitude can be described at its broadest as awareness of the presence of the Mystery and welcoming of its presence. By the term 'Mystery' I mean the reality that totally transcends human beings, while at the same time being intimately present within them: *interior intimo meo, superior summo meo*. This fundamental praying attitude has taken a multiplicity of forms in human history, ranging from the most crassly anthropomorphic representation of the Mystery to a form of representation that is radically apophatic or negative, in which the presence is only perceived as absent and the only word that can express it is silence.

This creates two major tendencies in the religions: the *prophetic* and the *mystical*, which cannot be described as entirely separate forms, because personal manifestations are never lacking in the predominantly mystical forms, nor are manifestations of apophatic and mystical spirituality in the predominantly prophetic forms. The prophetic religious tendency expresses awareness of the Mystery and our relationship with it in terms of an interpersonal relationship, dialogue, invocation, faith and confidence. The mystical religious tendency expresses this awareness and experiences this relationship in the form of meditation and concentration by the individual, culminating in absorption into the absolute or extinction – nirvana – in it.

In both traditions there is the awareness of a presence which makes worldly human reality ultimately unsatisfactory and polarizes it towards itself. In both, prayer is the exercise of the aspiration to transcendence inscribed in the human heart, which is the image of divinity and in movement towards it. In prophetic religions this is experienced as communication. In mystical religions it takes the form of communion.[10]

This fundamental praying attitude, experienced by different individuals in different circumstances and mental states, modulates into the various forms of prayer with which I began my description. Let us analyse in more detail petitionary prayer and thanksgiving, which for some writers, such as Calvin, constitute the two main classes or the two parts of prayer: *Orationis due sunt partes, petitio et gratiarum actio.*[11]

Petitionary prayer

This is the most widespread of prayer throughout the history of religions. Prayer so often takes the form of petition that quite a few definitions identify them and define prayer as asking God for appropriate things (*decentium*):[12] 'Praying is raising the heart to God and asking him for mercies.' The link between praying and petitioning seems so close that petition has been proposed as the original form of prayer from which all others derived.

The symphonic condition, to which I referred earlier, of all prayer and the discovery of forms called gratuitous in nearly all contexts, have enabled us to go beyond the evolutionary interpretations contained in these theories of prayer. But it is true that the prayer of petition is found in nearly all forms and stages of the religious life of humanity.

It is certainly present in the religious life of illiterate peoples and it has been called 'the simple prayer of primitive people'. In such prayers the worshipper asks for life, happiness, health, victory over enemies and every imaginable earthly good. The formulas are extraordinarily varied. They have a common structure in which we can distinguish principally the invocation of the divine being, the description of the situation of need or disaster in which the person praying stands and about which he or she complains, the sometimes very detailed listing of petitions and reasons why they should be heard, and the offering of intercessors to make the request more effective.[13]

Petitionary prayer also appears in polytheistic religions of the Vedic epoch and the great cultures of antiquity. The structure of its formulas is not fundamentally different, although the tone may be different in accordance with the religious and cultural differences. They also ask for long life, health, well-being and prosperity as in primitive prayer and often a votive formula is added to the petition to reinforce it and ensure its efficacy.'[14]

But the prayer of petition not only appears in primitive religions or at the primitive level of religious life. It is also present in the great monotheistic religions and, in highly purified form, in the prayer of the great religious geniuses. We need only refer to the insistent invitation to petition contained in the gospel teaching on prayer and the presence of petitions in both the official prayer (*salat*) and the private prayer (*d'ua'*) of Islam. The faithful Muslim repeats the petitions in the Qur'an for God's help, beginning with Sura 1, the *fatiha*, in which after praising the compassionate and merciful God, he prays: 'From you alone we implore help. Lead us in the right way.'[5]

Petition is not even totally absent from mystical religious prayer. Thus the Upanishads, especially when they are echoing Bhakti devotions, contain prayers like the following, which is often quoted:

> Lead me from non-being to being,
> Lead me from darkness to light,
> Lead me from death to immortality.[6]

Even in Buddhist prayer, as practised by the monks themselves in the Theravada, formulas appear expressing the desire for liberation, for the warding off of the consequences of evil actions, for progress along the road to illumination, without this meaning the establishment of a personal relationship with that higher reality to which they aspire. This reality is not thought of in terms of otherness from the human, and therefore in the strict sense the relationship assumed by petitionary prayer becomes impossible. Hence the specifically Buddhist form of prayer proper is meditation as a progress towards enlightenment – extinction in the absolute.[7]

The presence of this form of prayer in all world religions is explained by the fact that it is simply the result of recognizing the presence of the Mystery by human beings who are continually in need and, even in the most positive situations, cannot fail to perceive the distance between what they are and what they aspire to be. This gap between the being they are in fact and the ideal on the horizon of this being, is experienced as a need for salvation.

It is true that the formulas for petitionary prayer often betray a selfish attitude, a self-centredness which is in contradiction to the ecstatic and transcendent dimension contained in any authentic religious behaviour. This perversion of attitude also includes the perversion of petitionary prayer as a whole, the efficacy of which is now attributed to the mere recitation of a formula or the use of forms which are close to magic, by which it is believed that the higher power will be compelled to comply, and recourse to more or less subtle ways of winning this power's benevolence, with formulas of eulogy and praise, multiplying intercessors to help the prayer reach its target, currying favour with gifts, offerings and sacrifices, or rebuking and 'punishing' the gods who do not respond favourably to the demands of their worshippers.[18]

Hence the need was felt by those praying to purify their petitionary prayers. One way of doing this was to purify the objects of prayer, moving from asking favours of God to asking God's favour, which is his kindness and his presence. Above all the purification meant conforming to God's will and expressing confidence in it. Philosophical reflection as well as religious need sometimes contributes to this purification. Hence Socrates prays in these words: 'Zeus, grant us what is good, whether or not it is the object of our prayers, and keep us from what is evil, even if we ask you for it.'[19] And the Catholic liturgy asks: 'Grant your people to love what you ordain and desire what you promise, so that in the changes and chances of this world our hearts may be set where true joys are to be found.'[20]

Petitionary prayer reaches its most perfect expression in those formulas in which conformity to the will of the higher power shows an attitude of absolute confidence on the part of the worshipper, and also in other formulas – known as prayer of intercession and present in all traditions – in which the worshipper reminds the deity of the needs of other people and asks for help to respond to them.[21]

Prayer of thanksgiving and praise

Prayer of thanksgiving also appears in all religious contexts and at all stages of history. It has been said that in the prayer of primitive peoples and of the most unsophisticated worshippers, petitionary prayer predominates. It is the expression of a more utilitarian religious feeling. But now we know for certain that even these prayers contain gratuitous thanksgiving and praise. Proof of this are the numerous prayers in which worshippers address the higher powers to thank them, in general terms, for life, the kindness they have shown, or, in less abstract form, for giving favours asked for in a previous petition. 'Lord,' sings a fishing population in Ghana, 'this is the history of your mercy.'[22] A careful look at petitionary prayers shows that they are often associated with thanksgiving, as an introduction the function of which appears to be to capture God's benevolence, or as a conclusion. In fact there is hardly any petitionary prayer which does not also contain praise, including gratitude, just as there is hardly any prayer of praise that does not implicitly or explicitly contain petitionary prayer. Once more the principle is confirmed, to which I alluded earlier, of the synthetic or symphonic character of all authentic prayer.

However, there is no doubt that the prayer of thanksgiving is a special form of prayer with characteristic features manifesting new aspects of the common root, from which, like other forms of prayer, it grows. Let me try to point them out.[23]

In order to do this I think it is essential to refer first to the prayer of praise, with which thanksgiving is closely linked. The prayer of praise is the more original prayer form. Before talking about God, as the theologian does, or invoking God's help, as the person who petitions God does, the worshipper who praises God lets God speak through his voice or gestures, and thus speaks from God's standpoint or lets God speak through his or her prayer. For the prayer of praise does not consist primarily, as some of its formulas could show us, in attributing praises to God and making a panegyric. Fundamentally it consists in capturing the deity's greatness, holiness and beauty, and allowing this to be reflected in the worshippers' feelings, gestures, or voices. Hence the language appropriate to this prayer is that of admiration, which often uses superlatives, exclamations such as 'Oh!' and 'How great!', attempting to convey the excess with which the worshipper is overwhelmed. Therefore this prayer often also consists in 'making the deity great', that is, expressing in human words the greatness of God with which the worshipper has come into contact. Hence if prayer is the expression that comes closest to the religious attitude from which all other expressions arise, then the prayer of praise is the original form of prayer, because in it the religious attitude is expressed in 'explosive' form. Worshippers merely channel a current coming from beyond themselves which they are unable to control.[24] Hence, although the prayer of praise may take different forms, its most important literary form is the hymn, that is, a poetic composition in which affirmation, information and communication of content become secondary to the expression of a feeling produced by the breaking through of a reality the beauty, value and greatness of which surpass[25] the subject.

If petitionary prayer is the most faithful reflection of the human condition, with its limitations, anxieties and the calamities that life brings, the prayer of praise is the reflection in available human media or in nature, which is often associated with this prayer, of God's unutterable being.

We have well-known admirable Christian examples in the Song of the Creatures, the *Magnificat*, the *Gloria* and the *Sanctus* in the Mass, and the *Te Deum*. But this form of prayer is also present in all the great religions and is not lacking in the more popular manifestations of religion. We may recall that Islam frequently uses it in the form of *takbir*, 'Allah is great!', as the first part of the official prayer, *salat*, and in the form of *dikr*, a reminder and praise of Allah in the style of: 'Praise be to you, Allah! Yours be the praise! Blessed be your name! Exalted be your majesty! You alone are to be served!', in both official and private prayer.[26] We may also recall the hymns of praise with which Hinduism has continued the tradition of hymns present in the Vedas, in the forms of *stuti*, *strota* and *stava*, addressed to Vishnu, Shiva or Brahman, the absolute being.[27]

The formulas for the prayer of praise are very varied. Some take the form of blessing, expressing the worshipper's desire that the name of the deity be honoured. Others take the form of a grateful account of the wonders God has done in nature or in the lives of individuals or the people. At other times praise consists in recognizing God as the Lord on whom the worshipper depends, like a slave on his master or a subject on his prince. In some cases it takes the form of confession of faith, as happens in the strictly monotheistic professions of faith contained in Israel's *shema* in Judaism and in the *Sahado* or formulation of Muslim faith. On other occasions it is manifest in the attribution of countless honourable names to God: Allah's ninety-nine names, Vishnu's thousand names, the numerous names of the Buddha, especially in Mahayana Buddhism, or in the attribution to him of all thinkable perfections. Or in the enthusiastic repetition of God's name followed by victory exclamations such as Hosanna! Alleluia! Glory! Amen! and such like. Often words seem insufficient and the praise makes use of songs, the sound of musical instruments, gestures or dance.

Among these forms of praise, thanksgiving has its place, especially when it is not referring to particular goods which the divinity is asked for or has granted. Here the object of thanksgiving is God himself, his glory, his goodness or grace towards human beings. In my view, this particular form of prayer is situated between petitionary prayer, of which it frequently forms a part, and prayer of praise, in which it achieves its most perfect forms. If petitionary prayer particularly reflects the human conditions and the neediness in which we live, and if the prayer of praise is above all the reflection of the Mystery recognized by the religious, the prayer of thanksgiving expresses, with characteristic human ambiguity, the synthesis of finitude and infinity (Kierkegaard), human life as the reflection of God's glory from which it constantly proceeds.

Translated by Dinah Livingstone

Notes

1. Cf. the testimonies collected by F. Heiler in his book *Prayer. A Study in the History and Psychology of Religion*, Oxford 1932 [unfortunately this English translation is abridged and is missing much of the detailed material mentioned here. For that the reader must see the original, *Das Gebet*, Munich ⁵1923]. On the whole question cf. J. Martín Velasco, 'El hombre en oración. Actitud religiosa. Plegraria y condición humana', in *La Religión en nuestro mundo*, Salamanca 1978, 110–40; *Introducción a la fenomenología de la religión*, Madrid 1986, 172–184. See also A. González, *La Oración en la Biblia*, Madrid 1968, 17–67.

2. Cf. e.g. A. Sabatier, *Esquisse d'une philosophie de la religion* (1897), quoted by W. James, *The Varieties of Religious Experience*, 1902.

3. As an example of this variety of forms, cf. the summary listing some of them in Heiler, *Prayer* (n. 1), 353.

4. Cf. the comparative synoptic table of the degrees of prayer in different traditions and writers in Heiler, *Das Gebet* (n. 1) [not in the English translation].

5. As can be seen, here I attribute to every authentic form of prayer a quality that M. Nédoncelle, following L. Cognet, attributes to Christian prayer. M. Nédoncelle, *Prière humaine, prière divine*, Paris 1962, 144.

6. Cf. H. Limet's observation in H. Limet and J. Ries (eds.), *L'expérience de la prière dans les grandes religions*, Louvain-la-Neuve, Centre d'histoire des Religions, 1980, 15.

7. Heiler, *Prayer* (n. 1), 356.

8. Ibid.

9. Cf. M. Dhavamony, 'Hindu Prayer', in *Prayer-Prière*, *Studia Missionalia* 24, 1975, 185.

10. R. Bastide, 'L'expression de la prière chez les peuples sans écriture', *La Maison Dieu* 109, 1972, p. 120.

11. Quoted in Heiler, *Prayer* (n. 1), 271.

12. There is a list of numerous definitions of prayer in H. Bremond, *Introduction à la philosophie de la prière*, Paris 1929, 19–21.

13. Cf. Heiler, *Prayer* (n. 1), 15ff.; H. Huber, 'Das Gebet in den Naturreligionen', *Studia Missionalia* 24, 1975, pp. 39–44; A. Shorter, *Prayer in the Religious Traditions of Africa*, Nairobi, 1975, 21; L. Thomas and R. Luneau, *Les religions d'Afrique noire. Textes et traditions sacrées*, two vols., Paris ²1981. See also the chapter on prayer among peoples with an oral tradition in R. Boccassino (ed.), *La preghiera*, three vols., Milan and Rome 1967, Vol. 1, 43–198.

14. Cf. for example *Iliad* VI, 305–310. There are beautiful petitionary prayers from Egyptian religion in F. Daumas, 'L'expérience religieuse égyptienne dans la prière', in Limet and Ries (eds.), *Expérience de la prière* (n. 6), 59–80. On Hittite religion which was 'fundamentally self-interested and pragmatic', cf. R. Lebrum, 'Observations sur la prière hittite', ibid., 31–57.

15. Ary A. Roest Crollius, 'The prayer of the Qur'an', *Studia Missionalia* 24, 1975, 232, 236ff.

16. *Brihadaranyaka-Upanishad*, 1.3.1.

17. Cf. Marcelle Zago, 'La Preghiera nel Theravada Lao', and E. Paret, 'L'office quotidien dans les monastères du bouddhisme theravada', *Studia Missionalia* 24, 1975,

127–140, 141–163. See also G. R. Franci, 'La preghiera nelle religione indiane', in Boccassino (ed.), *Preghiera* (n. 13), 286–97.

18. Cf. examples of the latter in Heiler, *Prayer* (n. 17), 29ff.

19. Plato, *According to Alcibiades*, quoted in Nédoncelle, *Prière humaine* (n. 5), 131.

20. Collect for the Fourth Sunday after Easter.

21. There are many examples from 'primitive' populations in Heiler, *Prayer* (n. 1), 17ff. On the prayer of intercession in Islam, cf. Roest Crollius, 'Prayer of the Qur'an' (n.15), 236–40. The esteem in which this form of prayer is held in Judaism is well demonstrated by this sentence of the Talmud: 'Prayers for other people will be heard first', quoted in E. Wiesel, *Paroles d'étranger*, Paris 1982, 171.

22. Other examples in Shorter, *Religious Traditions* (n. 13), pp. 79–84.

23. Cf. A. di Nola, 'Preghiera', in *Enciclopedia delle religione*, Florence 1972, IV, 1775. A typical example of the threefold prayer of petition, thanksgiving and praise can be seen in *Iliad* 1, 453ff.

24. The term 'explosive' is used by J. Wach to speak of the original expressions of religious experience, *Vergleichende Religionsforschung*, Stuttgart, 1962, p. 79.

25. On the hymn and its relation to prayer cf. Heiler, *Das Gebet* (n. 1), he gives many examples taken from different religious contexts.

26. Cf. F. M. Pareja, *La Religiosidad musulmana*, Madrid 1975, 55ff. See also Roest Crollius, 'Prayer of the Qur'an' (n. 15), 227–32.

27. Cf. M. Dhavamony, 'Hindu Prayer', *Studia Missionalia* 24, 1975, 201–8.

Rabbinic *Berakhah* and Jewish Spirituality

Lawrence A. Hoffman

Jewish spirituality has known many forms. Hasidic Jews use wordless melodies. A popular Sabbath hymn, divided into four stanzas, each beginning with a different letter of the four-letter name of God, began as a private devotion by a mystic who, by his own testimony, stared at the letters until they merged together like a flaming fire. Many Jews to this day recite psalms when in distress, while others would insist that sitting around the Passover *seder* table, singing traditional folk songs with little or no theological import, is also a spiritual exercise. So too is the act of studying God's word.

But Judaism's multifaceted spiritual tapestry contains one common thread: the blessing, or benediction – in Hebrew the *berakhah*. The daily liturgy is constructed around blessings. Private spirituality, too, often calls for blessings, to the point where, it is said, the Nobel prize-winner, the author S. Y. Agnon, maintained that the greatest joy of receiving his coveted award was the fact that one of the world's few remaining kings presented it to him, thus giving him the chance to say an ancient benediction reserved for seeing kings: 'Blessed art Thou . . . who has shared His [sic][1] glory with mortals.' So too, a blessing precedes Talmud study, blessings mark the culmination of the marriage rite, blessings frame our meals, and blessings mark the imposition of sacred time as well as our encounter with sacred space.

As a literary category, the blessing is a rabbinic invention, largely completed by the third century of this era. As a theological desideratum, the blessing provides a window on the characteristic Jewish stance before God. This article seeks to explicate the spirituality implicit in the life of blessing.

The blessing defined

The blessing is a literary thing, a formula for couching words of prayer. The most obvious examples consist of short one-line introductions to diverse human experiences, everything from eating apples ('Blessed art Thou, Lord our God, ruler of the universe, who creates the fruit of the tree') to observing rainbows ('Blessed art Thou, Lord our God, ruler of the universe, who remembers the covenant [with Noah], who keeps covenantal faith, and who stands by His word'). Classical studies of this blessing genre identify its two units as a fixed-formula introductory *proclamation* in the second person ('Blessed art Thou . . .') followed by a variable specific-content clause – in this case, 'the *anamnesis* of the *mirabilia dei*' – in the third person (. . . who [does X]).[2]

A variation of this simple one-line blessing is the blessing one says upon performing a commandment. The fixed-formula introductory proclamation is, however, slightly altered so as to refer to commandments: 'Blessed art Thou, Lord our God, ruler of the universe, who has commanded us. . . .', but, like the prior pattern, the specific-content clause varies with the occasion: '. . . to kindle Sabbath lights' or '. . . concerning the eating of unleavened bread'. In any event, whether a blessing of enjoyment or of commandment, the elementary blessing is a one-line formula combining a fixed introduction and a variable conclusion.

Most blessings, however, are more complex. They have been expanded into theological essays on a given theme (creation or revelation, for example), ending with formulas that resemble the basic genre outlined above: 'Blessed art Thou, Lord, who creates the lights [of the heavens]' (for creation), and 'Blessed art thou, Lord, who loves His people Israel' (for revelation). This concluding formula is generally called a eulogy, though its Hebrew name *chatimah* is more aptly translated as 'seal'. Leading up to the eulogy is a lengthy 'body' that develops the thought which the eulogy then seals. Sometimes the body includes a petition, in which case the eulogy celebrates God's power to grant the request: for example, 'Heal us, Lord . . . Blessed art Thou, Lord, who heals the sick.' Some of these long benedictions begin with 'Blessed art Thou . . .' and others do not. But in any case, blessings are easily spotted as either simple one-line proclamations, or lengthy prose paragraphs with the requisite concluding eulogy.

Scholars have pondered the enigma of the blessing form, which changes from second to third person, as well as the history of its evolution.[3] What concerns us here is the blessing's remarkable success as a liturgical staple within Judaism. By the third century, if not earlier, the blessing form dominated every other literary style in Jewish worship. Biblical citations, for example, rarely occur alone in Jewish worship. Rather, they are cited within the blessing, as part of its thematic development; or, if they are read in their own right, they are usually introduced and/or concluded by blessings that justify them! Even the lectionary was so equipped, the Torah reading, for example, prefaced with a blessing celebrating revelation and concluding with a eulogy, 'Blessed art Thou, Lord, who gives the Torah.' Psalms, too, frequently take blessings before them – as in the celebrated recitation of *Hallel* Psalms (Pss. 113–118) at the Passover *seder*. Like a spiritual amoeba, the blessing incorporated all other worship forms, and in fact, in one occasion of note, it even forced a scriptural reading out of the worship service, and took its place instead.[4]

A third-century Palestinian authority, Rabbi Jochanan, is reported as holding, 'The men of the Great Synagogue [a catch-all term for authorities preceding the rabbis, but after the time of Ezra] instituted blessings [*berakhot*], prayers [*tefillot*], sanctifications [*kedushot*], and separations [*havdalot*] for Israel.' Originally, these must have been distinguishable as four differentiated liturgical entities, each with its own rules for structure and recitation.[5] But by Jochanan's time, the blessing's stature was such that the other three liturgical forms were couched in blessing style. The sanctification, for example, the forerunner of the *sanctus*, became a blessing on the theme of God's holiness, and was equipped with a eulogy, 'Blessed art Thou, Lord, the holy God'.

For good reason, the Mishnah (the formative statement of rabbinic thought dating from the end of the second century) has no section at all entitled 'Prayer' or 'Worship'. Its opening tractate, however, into which discussion of worship is embedded, is entitled 'Blessings'. By the second century, Rabbi Meir advised all Jews to say no less than 100 blessings every day. In sum, building on the Bible, but in their own creative way, the rabbis fashioned an entirely novel prose form that was so successful that it virtually became synonymous with Jewish worship in its entirety.

The blessing's function

But more than just a literary genre, the rabbinic blessing entails its own mode of spirituality. As we try to unravel it, we are immediately bedeviled by confusion entailed in translating the Hebrew into modern languages. To begin with, the standard call to prayer, which invites the assembly to *barekhu et adonai*, is usually translated as, 'Bless the Lord'.

Can people really 'bless' God, or does blessing necessarily flow the other way around?

In fact, however, translating the infinitive *levarekh* as 'To bless [God]' here is a mistake. Actually, the call to prayer invites people to do exactly what it says, namely, to pray – that is, to perform the variety of worship speech-acts which prayer entails. By worship speech-acts, I mean speech-acts that perform the functions of worship – such things as thanking God, praising God, entreating God, and so forth. But we have already seen that the prime speech-act for all worship functions is the blessing. The blessing is the rabbis' speech-carrier of choice, so to speak, the speech-act they preferred for all worship functions, including thanking, praising, and petitioning. Hence the call to prayer is not to be translated as 'Bless God', but 'Say blessings to God', which is another way of saying that the assembly should commence its public worship.[6]

The blessing does *not* function, then, as a human act of somehow conferring a blessed quality on God; at best, it is a recognition of God's status as already bless-ed, an affirmation that we already encountered in the fixed-formula introduction to the one-line benedictions and the eulogies: not 'We bless You', but 'Blessed art Thou' – in the sense that 'We affirm publicly that You, God, are bless-ed.'

Yet the blessing does not confer blessing on anything else either. When we say a blessing before eating bread, for example, we do not bless the bread; introducing the act of lighting Sabbath candles by a blessing does not add blessedness either to the act or to the candles. Secondary literature frequently presents the notion that Judaism urges us to sanctify the profane, partly through saying blessings; but this is the later theology of Kabbalistic and Hasidic thought. It is distinctly *not* early rabbinic spirituality.

Nor did the rabbis hold that through blessings, we at least invoke God's blessing on the objects in question. If we look carefully at the four typical occasions which evoke blessings, we will discover what the rabbis did believe blessings accomplish.

Occasions for blessing

Blessings may be divided into four categories:

1. *For performing comandments*: the occasions, mentioned above, which elicit the formula 'Blessed art Thou . . . who commanded us . . .'

2. *To punctuate time*: blessings that constitute the fixed liturgy for synagogue and home. These mark the daily schedule of the hours, as well as the annual calendar, with its feasts and fasts.

3. *To accompany some, but not all, voluntary acts*: eating, for example, or donning new clothes, or entering a cemetery. These are events we are called upon to do, some more often than others, but they remain elective, in that we plan them.

4. Related to 3, yet different, are *involuntary occasions* – again, not all, but some – which evoke blessings: seeing a rainbow, hearing good or bad news, or finding oneself at a place where a miracle occurred, for example. Unlike 3, these are events that come upon us unplanned.

I said above that blessings are not intended to bless something, in the sense of adding to its sanctity or conferring a sanctified state upon it. A closer analysis of category 3 will demonstrate, in fact, that just the opposite is the case. Rather than serving to confer sacrality on an otherwise profane item, the blessing actually removes the item in question from the realm of the sacred, so that human beings, who are not angels but humans, after all – and therefore mixtures of sacred and profane – may interact with it.

Blessings over elective acts: the case of food

For historical reasons too complex to go into here, food benedictions play a particularly large role in rabbinic spirituality.

The entire structure of blessings that accompany eating is discussed in the Mishnah's tractate 'Blessings', chapters 6–8. The three chapters in question are a carefully edited amalgam. Chapter 6 prescribes blessings before eating; Chapter 7 discusses the concluding grace, and Chapter 8 recounts differences of opinion on eating regulations between the two major schools of thought in the first century, the Hillelites and the Shammaites. Thus the editor proceeded logically from blessings prior to eating to blessings after eating, and finally, to some traditions regarding tableship meals in general.

We would expect the editor to have arranged each of the three chapters internally as well. Certainly Chapter 8 is so organized: its initial sentence is a summary statement introducing the rest of the tractate: 'These are the issues argued by the Shammaites and the Hillelites regarding meal rituals.' Similarly, Chapter 7 begins with the general instruction, 'Three who eat together are obliged to appoint one of their number to invite them all to say grace.' The opening statement of Chapter 6, however, appears at first glance to be a mere detail, for which the summary superscription is absent. It begins with the rhetorical question, 'What are the blessings to be recited for produce?' It then discriminates between produce from trees and produce from the earth, as follows:

(a) What blessing does one say over produce [*perot*]?
(b) Over produce of the tree, one says, '[Blessed art Thou . . .] who creates the produce of the tree.'
> (b1) except for wine, over which one says,
> '. . . who creates the produce of the vine'.
(c) Over produce of the earth, one says, '. . . who creates produce of the soil'.
> (c1) except for bread, over which one says, '. . . who brings forth bread from the earth'.
(d) for vegetables, one says, '. . . who creates the fruit of the soil'.
> (d1) Rabbi Judah says, '. . . who creates kinds of greenery'.[7]

Certainly from the perspective of modern readers who assume that the relevant overall consideration here ought to be the establishment of blessings for food *in general*; this opening paragraph appears to be only a set of details that ought more properly to have been subsumed under the more general question, 'What blessings does one say for food?' rather than 'What blessings does one say for produce?' Let us, however, read the paragraph with no prior bias regarding what the author ought to have done. Clearly the editor deliberately chose to introduce the chapter on blessings with a discussion of blessings over produce. The rest of the chapter, moreover, discusses special cases of produce, but never chicken, beef, or fish, for example. There are exceptions, but by and large, *it is not what humans make, but what the earth produces that dominates the author's attention*. Moreover, the blessing content invariably emphasizes the food's 'delivery system', that is, *how* a food comes to us from its source. Instead of construing the rabbininc editor's interest in produce as a sub-category of food in general, we should assume that for him, produce from the earth was the primary conceptual category. His concern was to provide blessings for the things we get from the earth, and to specify in each one the delivery-system, that is, how the food in question becomes available to us.

The theology behind this interest in the earth's produce is set forth in two remarkably straightforward rabbinic texts.

It is written, 'The earth is the Lord's and the fullness thereof' (Ps. 24.1), but we read also, 'God has given the earth to human beings' (Ps. 115.16). There is no contradiction. The first verse reflects the situation before we say a blessing, and the second verse refers to after the blessing has been said.[8]

In other words, *food blessings function to release food of the earth from its natural state of belonging to God*. No wonder these blessings expressly state the food's delivery system! The whole point of saying them is to effect the delivery of food to humans, to go from Psalm 24.1 to Psalm 115.16, as the Talmud puts it.

A variant version of the same teaching instructs us,

One should eat nothing before saying a blessing, as it is written, 'The earth is the Lord's and the fullness thereof' (Ps. 24.1). One who makes enjoyable use of this world without a blessing is guilty of sacrilege [*me'ilah*].[9]

'Sacrilege' here is the rabbinic term describing the use by laypeople of that which belongs to the Temple. It is the act of enjoying *hekdesh* ('sacred property') by people who are themselves not in a state of *kedushah*, 'sanctity'. In other words, far from *adding* sanctity to what we eat, blessings over food *release what we eat from its natural state of sanctity, so that we, who are not God, can eat it in the first place*.[10]

Blessings as transformative

Blessings over food are thus transformative. They are recited at the liminal boundary between ourselves and food which belongs to God, and thus is *hekdesh*, and beyond human reach. Food blessings are thus *speech-acts that transform the sacred into the profane*, so that ordinary people can consume it. At issue here is the primary binary opposition that motivates the entire rabbinic system: sacred and profane [*kodesh/chol*].[11] By rabbinic logic, all aspects of the cosmos must be measured by the relative degree of sanctity they contain. Space, for example, can be completely sacred (the holy of holies at the Jerusalem Temple) or somewhat less holy (the temple courtyard) or a little less sacred than that (the Land of Israel); by contrast, however, space outside the Land of Israel is not sacred at all.[12] Similarly, ordinary time (Sunday to Friday) is not sacred, but Sabbaths and festivals are fully sacred, while New Moons and intermediate days of festivals are half-holy days, somewhere in between. The rabbis thus give us a *graded system of sacrality*, for time, space, people and things.

One function of rabbinic rite is to do away with anomalies in holiness. Priests, for example, are holier than Israelites. An Israelite who has a first-born son must deal with the anomaly of a child who – by biblical decree – belongs to God, and thus is too sacred to function as the Israelite he is. The priests are to own him. But, not being a priest, he cannot function within the priestly caste either. Such a child is thus to be redeemed from his sacred status, and freed to live a normal life.[13] In the rabbinic rite of redemption, a blessing brings about this trans-formation.[14] A more regular, but related, function of rabbinic ritual is to help the ordinary Jew deal with the fact that he or she is asked to live in a time-space universe where the degree of holiness varies. Again, it is blessings which help one cross the liminal boundary between one degree of sacrality and another. We thus return to the categories of blessing cited above. All of them can be explained as attempts to cross holy/profane boundaries.

In category 3, we saw how food blessings operate. Other cases involve acts like entering sacred space (a cemetery) or wearing new clothes, a making-present of the divine act of clothing the naked. As such, no less than when we eat God's produce, these acts put us in contact with the sacred, and thus, they require blessings. Category 4 is similar: it consists of sacred space or cosmic events that intrude upon us. We see a rainbow, observe a storm, or greet a monarch. To the rabbinic mind, these are all reflections of God's promise, might, or glory – as the blessings themselves say. So we open ourselves to them by removing them from the category of pure sacrality and, like the food we eat, render them fit for human enjoyment. Similarly, the normal public liturgy of category 2 can be explained as the intrusion into our lives of the flow of time. It is God who brings on day and night, the blessing says – again, an explicit reference to the delivery system, this time not of food, but of cosmic phenomena that are delivered to our senses, and must be *de*sanctified if we are to enjoy them. Alternatively, there are the blessings for the Sabbath and holy days, not in order to sanctify them – for they are already holy – but to enable Israel to partake of them, insofar as Israel is a sacred people. And finally, there are the blessings over commandments, which make it possible for ordinary Jews to do God's work.

Mircea Eliade held that religion enables human beings to re-enact hierophanies, the moments in history when the divine broke in upon us. For the rabbis, the divine regularly breaks in upon us: in sacred time, sacred space, representations of sacred events, God's daily work in the heavens, and even ordinary human activities that take on sacred status by virtue of their being commanded at Sinai. All of these take blessings. *First and foremost, blessings are the liturgical speech-act that celebrates hierophany, opening the Jew to the possibility of crossing the border into the realm of the sacred.*

The life of blessing: standing before God in thanksgiving and praise

Concepts are often best handled through exploring their 'spectrum'. I have in mind the phenomenon that for every word, illustrative of a concept, there is a spectrum of situations marked by the degree to which the concept is present, ranging from not at all to very much indeed. A concept can thus be arrayed in what I will call a 'conceptual spectrum' going from one pole to another, with the two poles being opposites. Heuristically, now, we label the oppositions entailed in a comparison of the entries at each of the two ends. The following chart illustrates what I have in mind:

(*a*) Particularism/universalism
(*b*) individual as partner with God/individual as dependent before God
(*c*) 'acknowledgement' of 'other' as equal/'thanksgiving' to 'other' as superior
(*d*) *pro*fession of merit/*con*fession of sin

By analysing these two poles of experience, we arrive at a two-fold model of spirituality. We shall see that rabbinic Judaism participates in both; and that the two poles come together in the theology of blessing.

In (*a*), we have the well-known tension between the particularistic perception of Jewish existence, by which the Jew is a member of the chosen people, and the universalistic perception of oneself as a member of the human race.

The universalistic anthropology reflects our self-consciousness as human beings in the state of nature. Without the covenant, people deserve nothing, and are appropriately grateful for anything God gives them. When I say the right-side pole is universalistic, then, I do not mean to imply that Jews characterize non-Jewish communities that way; it is not as if only Jews have a particularistic covenant, while others do not, so are at a disadvantage before God. On the contrary, the rabbinic concept of the Noahide covenant by which God is presumed to have covenanted also with Noah as the paradigmatic non-Jew, rescues everyone (potentially) from the status of merely universal species. By universalism, I mean the perspective according to which any man or woman is just man or woman, a member of no community at all. It is the philosopher's state of nature, presumed to precede human community.

No less than the philosophers, Judaism too values community. Rather than a *social* contract, however, Judaism postulates a *divine* contract: God met Israel at Sinai, and other peoples on their own ground, to make communal covenants. Ever after, individuals are members of peoples, with callings, purpose, and rights which the contract stipulates. On the other hand, from time to time, members of all communities, Jews included, must see themselves as the naked men and women they are, and in that guise, they stand alone as universals, suddenly aware how little they matter, how sinful they are, how groundless are their rights before God, and how grateful they should be for everything they have.

Thus, in (*b*), from the universalistic premise, we get an anthropology of total dependence on God. But from the particularistic stance, where we meet God as a covenanted partner, we are not dependent on God's grace alone. To be sure, the covenant itself may be construed as a gift of grace, but having been given, it alters the status of its recipient; we may now claim rights unavailable so long as the sole human status available was universal man/woman. In the first instance, on the chart's right side, the Jew stands before God as a mere human creature before a mighty creator. In the second and opposite case, one receives God's gifts, but not as gifts, so much as one's covenantal due.

In (*c*), we see the two poles of consciousness resulting in two usages of the verb *ydh*. Sometimes the verb is used in the sense of offering thanks, while on other occasions, it is employed as 'to acknowledge'. These are not identical ideas. The former use generally 'thanks' God for what we, as human beings, have received. At such moments we stand in absolute awe at God's gifts wholly beyond our merit. This is the spirituality of grace, generating only profound thanksgiving to God who enriches us far beyond our worth. But in so far as we stand in covenant with God, seeing God as a partner, it is not so much absolute gratitude that is evoked as it is praiseful acknowledgment of God who, in fact, asks precisely that of Israel, the covenanted partner. The difference in the two perspectives and their integration in Jewish spirituality can be readily seen in the following prayer, drawn from *Seder Rav Amram*, our first-known instance of a comprehensive prayer book, dated to the middle of the ninth century. This is an early morning prayer, in which the Jew arises from sleep, conscious of existing as a universal human being, who might well have died during the night, but who miraculously awakens, breathes again, watches the sun come up, and thanks God for existence itself. But by the second paragraph, the tone changes. The Jew reflects on the fact that mortality has been graced with covenantal meaning, and the prayer of thanks is transformed into a prayer of praise.

Master of all worlds, we cast our supplications before You, not on account of our own righteousness, but because of Your great mercy. What are we, what is our life, what is our compassion, what is our righteousness, what is our strength? What can we say before You, Lord our God? Are not all the mighty as nothing before You, and those of renown as though they had never existed, the sages as if they were without knowledge, and the discerning as if without insight. For all our deeds are an 'unformed void' [*tohu vavohu*], and the days of our lives are vanity before You. As scripture says, 'Humans are no better than animals, for all is vanity' (Eccles. 3.19).

But we are Your covenanted people, children of Abraham who loved You, with whom You made a sacred oath on Mt Moriah; descendants of Your precious Isaac who was bound on the altar; the congregation of Jacob, Your first-born son, whom You named Israel and Jeshurun on account of Your love for him and Your joy in him. Therefore, we are obliged to acknowledge You with praise, by saying daily before You: how happy we are, how good is our portion, how lovely is our lot, how fine is our inherited tradition whereby, regularly, every morning and evening, we affirm, 'Hear O Israel, The Lord is our God, the Lord is One!'[5]

Finally, in (*d*) we arrive at the reflexive mood (the *hitpa'el*) of the root in question (*ydh*), *lehitvadot*, which means 'to make confession'. The nominal form *vidui*, 'confession', is the title of the prayer in which Jews customarily confess their sins: a liturgical staple for the High Holy Day period. But closer inspection demonstrates (in [*d*]) that the *vidui* as *con*fession exists only as one extreme of the conceptual spectrum, namely, the right-hand side where we are aware of our creatureliness, our inferiority before God, our dependence on God's grace for our gifts, and thus, the extent to which we are really unworthy of all that God gives us. At the other end of the line, one would hardly expect to find emphasis on the negative side of human nature, for there, God exists in covenant with men and women who deserve what they receive.

In fact, the earliest notion of *vidui* means not *con*fession but *pro*fession, a calling to mind of the positive fulfilment of our covenantal obligation: that is, the *pro* not the *con*. It occurs in the Bible (Deuteronomy 26) and in the Mishnah with regard to the profession of the second tithe. The latter text demonstrates that farmers in the first century still recited the Bible's mandated formula – as we would expect – but fortunately, the Mishnah's editor has glossed the farmers' ritualized profession with his own exegetical commentary on what he thought it meant. Particularly in the last line, we find incontrovertible evidence that the *vidui* was a *pro-* not a *con*fession. 'I have done everything You have commanded me,' he declares (following Deut. 26.14) with pride unbecoming the attitude we would expect of a confessant! And then, lest we suspect that the words are mere formulaic ritualization, their plain sense unintended, the Mishnah's editor adds: '[This means,] We have done everything You ordained for us; now You do what You promised us.'[6] Clearly, we have no penitent cowering in the shadow of the Almighty here, no accent on grace and sin, but the left side of the spectrum emphasizing covenant and dues mutually expected and mutually given between God and Israel.[7]

Blessings as reflective of both poles

Jewish spirituality bids us be conscious of both poles of existence, our universalistic dependence on God's grace, and our covenanted status as well. As the Jew's dominant mode of interaction with the realm of the sacred, the blessing reflects both poles of relationship.

By themselves, after all, blessings are just speech acts, prose formulas in which any content may be cast. By and large, categories 3–4 lie in the universalistic side of the spectrum. In 3, as humans dependent on food and drink, we release the earth's bounties for our enjoyment; in 4, we behold the staggering cosmos of thunder, majesty, rainbows and blossoms – all instances of God's activity in a world where there are no covenants yet. This is our apprehension of the raw state of the sacred; it is Otto's numinous, before which we stand in full regard of our mere 'creatureliness'.

But category 1 is the Jew's affirmation of the covenant; a series of blessings said because we have been commanded to do such and such by virtue of our covenantal state. It is praise now, not thanksgiving, which is the dominant perspective of the covenanted community. And category 2 is a mixture of both, sometimes a reflection on the passage of time from the point of view of every-man or -woman – God's rolling back the darkness with the morning light – and sometimes from the perspective of covenanted Israel – as in the annual unfolding of Israel's sacred calendar.

Blessings, then, are the Jew's primal act of worship, containing within them the two approaches to the world that the Jew respects as necessary for the realization of the Jewish life of faith.

Notes

1. Current translations avoid exclusive language for God, for example replacing 'His' with 'Your'. In this article, I translate literally from the classical texts.
2. J. -P. Audet, 'Literary Forms and Contents of a Normal *Eucharistia* in the First Century', *Studia Evangelica*, Berlin 1959, p. 646.
3. See Joseph Heinemann, *Prayer in the Talmud*, Berlin and New York 1977.
4. Originally, the Ten Commandments were read each morning and evening. By the middle of the second century, a blessing on revelation was said in their place.
5. See Lawrence A. Hoffman, *Beyond the Text: a Holistic Approach to Liturgy*, Bloomington, Indiana 1987, pp. 28–30.
6. For a detailed account, see Lawrence A. Hoffman, 'Blessings and their Translations in Current Jewish Liturgies', *Worship* 60, March 1986, pp. 134–61, esp. 153–8. Cf. José Faur, 'Delocutive Expressions in the Hebrew Liturgy', *Journal of Ancient Near Eastern Studies* 16–17, 1984–1985.
7. M. Ber. 6.1. The standard translation is now Jacob Neusner, *The Mishnah: a New Translation*, New Haven and London 1988. Unless indicated here, translations are my own, though I borrow insights regularly from Neusner, as, for example, the translation of *perot* here as 'produce', rather than the usual 'fruit'.
8. Ber. 35a.
9. T. Ber. 4.1. For full discussion of this and parallel texts, see Baruch M. Bokser, '*Ma'al* and Blessings over Food: Rabbinic Transformation of Cultic Terminology and Alternative Modes of Piety', *JBL* 100, 1981, 558–70.
10. For further detail, see Lawrence A. Hoffman, 'Land of Blessing and Blessings of the Land,' in id. (ed.), *Land of Israel: Jewish Perspectives*, Notre Dame, Indiana 1986, 1–23.
11. For detail, see Hoffman, *Beyond the Text* (n.5), ch. 2.
12. M. Kelim 1.6–9; see Richard S. Sarason, 'The Significance of the Land of Israel in the Mishnah', in Hoffman, *Land of Israel* (n.10), 109–36.
13. See Numbers 18.15–16.
14. Manuscript evidence provides early Palestinian blessings that have dropped out of our present-day rite: for example, 'Blessed art Thou, who sanctifies the first-born of Israel, for[?] their redemptions'. The final preposition varies. Cf. texts in B. M. Lewin, *Otsar Hageonim*, Vol. 3, 130, and Israel Ta-Shema, 'Addendum', in M. Margoliot, *Hilkhot Erets Yisra'el*.
15. *Seder Rav Amram*, Goldschmidt ed., p. 10.
16. See Deut. 26 for the biblical basis of this *vidui*; and M. Maaser Sheni 5.10–13 for the text of the farmers' ritualized statement in the first century CE.
17. See discussion and notes in Hoffman, *Beyond the Text* (n. 5), 79–82.

Speaking to 'Abba': Prayer as Petition and Thanksgiving in the Teaching of Jesus

George M. Soares-Prabhu

'Christianity,' Lucien Cerfaux reminds us, 'did not come into the world as an explosion of prayer.'[1] The world of Jesus, both the Jewish world in which he lived and the larger Hellenistic world of which it was an integral but unassimilated part, was rich in the forms and formulae of prayer. The New Testament had little to add to this. It contributed nothing to the splendid sacrificial liturgy of the Second Temple, nor to the immense 'treasure house of . . . prayers of imperishable worth',[2] stored up in the Psalter of the Hebrew Bible; nor to the secret but profoundly moving rites which led the initiates of the mystery religions to their blissful experience of salvation. Compared to all this (and even more when compared to the vast wealth and variety of the rituals, meditation techniques and forms of prayer that Hinduism has to offer),[3] New Testament teaching on prayer is meagre indeed!

I. Getting to know the teaching of Jesus on prayer

This teaching goes back to Jesus, whose own experience of prayer is the basis of what the New Testament teaches. For in spite of the great variety of traditions in the New Testament, orientations on prayer remain strikingly unchanged all through the book. John has obviously (re)formulated the prayers of Jesus in the light of his own theology of glory. We see this when we look at the typically Johannine vocabulary of the prayer of Jesus at the tomb of Lazarus (John 11.41f.); or when we compare the 'Johannine Gethsemane' (John 12.27f.) with that of the Synoptics (Mark 14.36); or Jesus' prayer of thanksgiving in John (John 17.1–26) with his thanksgiving in Matthew (Matt. 11.25f.). Both the Synoptic prayers of Jesus (petition and thanksgiving) are thus to be found in John, though in an altered form! Again, John gives an explicitly christological colouring ('in my name') to Jesus' instruction that we ask God for what we need (John 14.13; 15.16; 16.23). But the Johannine sayings are clearly related to those in the Synoptics, because their basic form (the 'ask and you will receive' of John 16.24) obviously echoes the 'ask and it will be given to you' of the Synoptics (Matt. 7.7 = Luke 11.9).[4] In Paul too, though the emphasis shifts from petition to thanksgiving,[5] the basic structure of Christian prayer (moving from confident petition to joyous thanksgiving) remains unchanged. And the instructions on the efficacy of petitionary prayer that we find in I John 3.22 ('we receive from him whatever we ask'), and in James 1.5 ('if any one of you lacks wisdom, let him ask God . . . and it will be given to him') are so similar to the Q saying in Matt 7.7 = Luke 11.9 ('ask and it will be given to you') that we surely have here a tradition which has been transmitted with great fidelity all through New Testament times.

We find in the various books of the New Testament, then, a unified and consistent teaching on prayer; and this is best explained by assuming that this teaching is the result of a developing but basically undistorted tradition, which goes back to Jesus himself. Access to the origins of this tradition (the teaching of Jesus) is provided by the Synoptic Gospels, whose teachings on prayer reproduce a very early stage of it. We may with some confidence, then, rely on the Synoptic Gospels to tell us what Jesus taught about prayer.

The Synoptic Gospels give us 1. the text of three prayers recited by Jesus at peak moments in his life: his glad cry of thanksgiving at the return of his disciples from their successful mission (Luke 10.21f. = Matt. 11.25f.); his anguished petition for a reprieve from his approaching death at Gethsemane (Mark 14.36 = Matt. 26.39 = Luke 2.42); and his cry of abandonment on the cross (Mark 15.34 = Matt. 27.46).[6] They also describe 2. a model prayer which Jesus taught his disciples as 'their' prayer (Luke 11.2–4 = Matt. 6.9–13). And they hand down 3. instructions on prayer (sayings and parables) given by Jesus, in which Jesus does not spell out a method for praying (as an oriental *guru* would do) but tells us what to pray for, and what attitude to adopt when praying. We are to pray for the Kingdom (Luke 11.2), which comes as the fulfilment of all our needs (Matt. 6.33); and we are not to pray ostentatiously like the Pharisees (Matt. 6.5f.), nor wordily like the Gentiles (Matt. 6.7f.), but with an attitude of faith (Mark 11.24 = Matt. 21.22), of forgiveness (Mark 11.25), of tireless perseverance (Luke 18.1–8) and of oneness in community (Matt. 18.19f.).

II. The basis of the teaching of Jesus on prayer

Here, precisely, lies the distinctive feature of Jesus' teaching on prayer. Jesus does not give us a new form of prayer – except for the Lord's Prayer, which is more a model than a formula. He himself and his followers after him continue (to this day) to use the prayer forms of the Hebrew Bible, specially the Psalms. Nor does he elaborate new techniques for praying. Prayer techniques are poorly developed in Christianity (as compared to, say, Hinduism or Buddhism), and where they exist they are usually merely the accumulated experience of generations of praying Christians, put together without much rigour.[7] Instead, what Jesus gives us is a new attitude in prayer, emerging out of a new experience of God. All Jesus' prayer, and all his teaching on prayer, flows out of his experience of God as *abba*. It is this which explains the specific orientation of the prayer of Jesus, and its disconcerting neglect of 'technique' in favour of 'attitude'.

For Jesus experiences God not as the all-pervading Absolute (*brahman*) who is the real 'self' (*ātman*) of the cosmos and of every individual thing in it, but as the loving Parent (*abba*) who has gifted itself in love to humankind. God is therefore to be encountered not through 'meditation', that is, through a sustained introspective awareness that leads to the perception of 'the Self in the self' (*Bhagvadgita* vi.20); but through 'prayer', that is, through an inter-personal 'conversation' with God, in which love is experienced and given, and relationships of intimacy are founded.[8] Meditation may need highly refined techniques. But techniques are not usually helpful in a conversation, except perhaps at the start, to set the conversation going. Once that is done, the dynamics of personal interaction take over, and what is needed is not a technique but an attitude of mutual openness and trust.

The basic attitude which Jesus looks for in his followers at prayer has been imaged by him in the figure of a child. 'Truly I say to you,' he says solemnly, 'whoever does not receive the Kingdom of God like a child, shall not enter it' (Mark 10.15 = Luke 18.17). To receive the Kingdom of God like a child means to accept God's saving love with the openness, the trust, the freedom and the spontaneity with which a child responds to life. It means to accept fully (as children do) the giftedness of life – not to count on one's merits like the Pharisee at prayer in the parable of Jesus (Luke 18.9–14), nor to cling to one's posessions like the rich man who wants to follow

Jesus in the Gospel story (Mark 10.17–22),[9] but to be simple, unself-righteous, trusting and free.

Jesus requires this attitude of his followers because it is the obverse side of the specific experience of God he has given them. To the foundational Christian experience of God as a loving Parent (*abba*), there corresponds (dialectically) the basic Christian attitude of receiving the Kingdom like a child. To the on-going Christian experience of God's absolute paternal, or better, maternal, care (for it is the mother not the father who feeds and clothes), there corresponds (dialectically) the continuing Christian attitude of a carefree and childlike trustfulness that does not worry about the morrow (Matt. 6.25–34). Experience and attitude are thus related to each other, dialectically. God is experienced as a loving and a caring parent only when we receive the Kingdom of God (God's saving love) like a trusting child; but we can receive the Kingdom of God like a child only when we have experienced the provident love of God.

It is from this dialectic of experience and attitude that Christian prayer emerges. Because the Christian experiences God as a loving parent and relates to God as a trusting child, Christian prayer will be a child's prayer. Such prayer will be primarily a prayer of petition and of thanksgiving, because asking and thanking (specially asking) are normal forms in a child's conversation. We understand, then, why the teaching of Jesus on prayer, as revealed in the Synoptic Gospels, insists so strongly on petition and (to a lesser extent) on thanksgiving.

III. Petition in the teaching of Jesus

(a) The Lord's Prayer

When his disciples ask Jesus to teach them to pray (Luke 11.2), he does not give them a technique for praying but, typically, teaches them a prayer of petition (Matt. 6.9–13 = Luke 11.2–4). In its original form, as uttered by Jesus, the prayer would have probably sounded as follows:[10]

> Abba!
> May your name be holy,
> May your kingdom come;
> Our bread for tomorrow, give us today.
> Forgive us our debts as we now forgive our debtors;
> And do not allow us to fall away from you.

The prayer begins by addressing God as *abba*, and so setting the tone for the familial mood of the 'conversation' which is to follow. The confidence expressed and engendered by this intimate form of address leads smoothly to the five petitions of the prayer. Of these the first two, the so-called 'you-petitions', ask the Father to make his name holy and to allow his Kingdom to come – parallel ways of saying the same thing. They prepare for the three so-called 'we-petitions' that follow. This they do in two ways. The first of the 'you-petitions' ('may your name be holy') can be read as a form of acknowledgment and praise, which in a prayer of petition could serve to dispose God to respond favourably to the petitions that follow. More significantly, the second 'you-petition' ('may your kingdom come') prays for the realization of God's eschatological salvation, the concrete dimensions of which are then spelled out in the three 'we-petitions' that follow. In these we pray for our 'bread for tomorrow' (that is, for physical and spiritual sustenance); for the forgiveness which, we acknowledge, is dialectically related to our forgiving people who have injured us (that is, for a right relationship with God and with 'neighbour'); and for preservation from the threat of apostasy (that is, for lasting fidelity to God). In the three 'we-petitions' we thus pray for the concrete realization of the new eschatological existence in love given to us by Jesus (the Kingdom), in the economic, social and religious areas of our lives. It would be difficult to find a prayer which says so much so briefly. The prayer is short, simple, comprehensive and profound.

This extraordinary prayer taught by Jesus to his disciples is truly the 'Lord's Prayer'! It reveals the structure of Jesus' own understanding of what prayer is. All his teaching on prayer must therefore be understood in its light. But the Lord's Prayer, like all Jesus' teaching and preaching, in word and in deed, is centred wholly on the Kingdom. It is in terms of the Kingdom, then, that the prayers Jesus says, and the instructions on prayer that he gives, are to be understood.

(b) Jesus' instructions on prayer

In the Synoptic Gospels, the instructions of Jesus on prayer (as distinct from the prayers he says, or the model-prayer he gives) can be put together in four groups. There are: 1. three Lucan parables (the Friend at Midnight in Luke 11.5–8; the Importunate Widow in Luke 18.1–8; and the Pharisee and the Tax-Collector in Luke 18.9–14), which urge us to pray insistently, and with humility, in the confident assurance that our prayer will be heard, because it is addressed to a God who cares for us much more than any human friend; 2. a pair of sayings in Mark which teach the need of praying with faith if our petition is to be heard (Mark 11.24 = Matt. 21.22), and with forgiveness if our own sins are to be forgiven (Mark 11.25); 3. a saying in Matthew (Matt. 18.19f.), which assures us that the 'Father in heaven' will grant anything asked for by 'two or three' gathered together in the name of Jesus; and 4. two sayings from Q, one of which (Matt. 9.37 = Luke 10.2) is an apocalyptic exhortation urging us to pray that God may send us helpers for the promising eschatological mission entrusted to us, while the other (Matt. 7.7–11 = Luke 11.9–13) is a well-formulated wisdom admonition recommending petitionary prayer.

Of all these it is the last, the Q wisdom admonition, that is the most interesting and important, because it provides us with a compact but comprehensive summary of Jesus' own teaching on prayer of petition. The prayer parables in Luke (which probably also go back to Jesus himself) give us powerful confirmatory illustrations of what the admonition teaches, but they add nothing new. Nor do the sayings on prayer in Matthew and Mark (probably community creations), because they are merely concrete applications of this teaching to specific situations in the early Church. It is the admonition in Matthew's Sermon on the Mount (Matt. 7.7–11 = Luke 11.9–13) that tells us most clearly what Jesus has to say about petitionary prayer.

In its original form the Q admonition would probably have read:[11]

A. Ask and it will be given to you
   Seek and you will find
   Knock and the door will be opened to you.
B. For everyone who asks receives,
   And one who seeks, finds,
   And to the one who knocks the door will be opened.
C. Who is the person among you,
   who when his son asks him for a loaf of bread
      will give him a stone?
   Or when he asks him for a fish
      will give him a snake?
   If then you, being evil,
      know how to give good gifts to your children,
   How much more will your Father in heaven
      give good things to those who ask him?

The passage is beautifully structured. It begins (A) with a thrice repeated exhortation (ask-seek-knock) to petitionary prayer. The exhortation is motivated (B) through a thrice repeated assertion that petition will always be answered. Exhortation and motivation are parellel but not tautologous, because the emphasis shifts from petition ('ask') in A to the concession of the petition ('you will receive') in B. The admonition concludes (C) by setting out the ultimate theological basis for the efficacy of petitionary prayer. Two parallel illustrations from everyday life, formulated as a pair of rhetorical questions, build up an *a fortiori* argument, which argues from the experienced benevolence of human parents (who will not give their children a stone instead of a loaf of bread, or a snake instead of a fish) to the much greater readiness of God to give 'good things' to those (God's children!) who ask for them.

With its well-rounded structure, its authoritative tone, its rootedness in the experience of God as *abba*, its parabolic form and rhythmic style, and its close agreement with the social and linguistic milieu of pre-70 CE Judaism, this wisdom admonition is a unit which has all the marks of being an authentic saying of Jesus. It draws our attention to the great importance given to petition in the teaching of Jesus on prayer. Indeed, almost all the sayings on prayer reported in the Synoptic Gospels are about prayer of petition; so that 'to pray' (*proseuchesthai*) in the Gospels is almost synonymous with 'to ask' (*aitein, deisthai, erotan, parakalein*). Such prayer, Jesus assures us, is always effective. Its effectiveness is affirmed repeatedly in formulations which shock us by their forcefulness. 'Everyone who asks receives', says Jesus, with a categorical firmness that allows no restriction of limit or condition. His affirmation that prayer is heard is as universal and as absolute as it could possibly be.

Elsewhere in the Gospels conditions sometimes occur: rarely in the Synoptics (Mark 11.24; Matt. 18.19f.), generally in John (14.13, 15.16; 1 John 3.22).[12] These are usually prudential comments of the early church, which tone down, but do not take away, the radicalness of Jesus' affirmation. What they tell us is that the efficacy of petitionary prayer is enhanced by insistent perseverance in prayer (Luke 18.1–8), carried out in an attitude of a faith so trusting that it believes that the petition prayed for has already been granted (Mark 11.24), and supported by a community consensus (Matt. 18.19f.). But the efficacy of petitionary prayer is not dependent on these dispositions of the person praying. It derives, ultimately, wholly from the benevolence of God who, because God is *abba*, gives 'good things' to all those who ask. The dispositions mentioned in the Gospels as 'conditions' for efficacious prayer do not, in fact, dispose God to give: they dispose the one who asks to receive.

(c) The problem of unanswered prayer

Such teaching on prayer of petition poses a problem, which is experienced by all those who pray, and which has often been expressed with great poignancy in the prayers of mystics and saints. It is the problem of unanswered prayer. If everyone who asks receives, how is it that so many (often those most in need) do not get what they pray for? Is not the teaching of Jesus unrealistic here – the expression of a primitive, childish naiveté, rather than of a mature if childlike faith, appropriate to a world come of age? In part, an answer is given by Jesus himself. For his prayer in Gethsemane is a dramatic example of unanswered prayer. The way Jesus prays here suggests that all the prayer of petition he commends contains (like his own prayer) an unstated condition, 'not what I will but what you will' (Mark 14.36). We respond to God's unconditional love for us by placing in God a trust so absolute that our prayer is always 'Your will be done'. For God's will, we believe, is indeed our peace.

To put it in another way, all Jesus' teaching on petitionary prayer is to be understood in the light of the Lord's Prayer, which, I have suggested, determines the horizon of Jesus' own understanding of prayer. But the Lord's Prayer is wholly prayer for the Kingdom. When, therefore, Jesus exhorts us to ask, to seek and to knock, it is not for casual 'favours' that he wants us to pray. He is urging us to pray for the Kingdom of God (his sole preoccupation), which, as the new existence in love gifted to us by God, does in fact fulfil every aspiration of human life. Like the petitions of the Lord's Prayer, all our petitions are ultimately paraphrases of the one great petition: 'May your kingdom come.' As such, they are always answered – but in God's way, not in ours, as Mahatma Gandhi has aptly said.[13] God does indeed give 'good things' (the blessings of the Kingdom) to all those who ask (Matt. 7.11).

IV. Thanksgiving in the teaching of Jesus

Prayer, understood as petition, is often associated with thanksgiving in the New Testament. This is specially so in Paul. His letters almost always begin with a thanksgiving, which is part of the normal form of a letter in the Hellenistic world, but which Paul usually expands well beyond conventional limits to express his overflowing gratitude (Phil. 1.3–11; I Thess. 1.2–10). And his letters often end with an exhortation to 'pray constantly' and 'give thanks in all circumstances' (I Thess. 5.17f. – cf. Phil. 4.6; I Tim. 2.1), through which he attempts to draw his readers into his spirituality of continual petition and thanksgiving.

This association of petition and thanksgiving is not accidental. It reflects the close relationship that exists between these two streams of prayer, both of which emerge from the same basic attitude of childlike faith with which the followers of Jesus respond to the revelation of God as *abba*. This attitude implies both an awareness of our powerlessness to merit love (so that we are driven to 'ask' for the Kingdom), and the awareness that love has been freely gifted to us by God (so that we are moved to thank God for the 'good things' we have been given). Prayer of thanksgiving in the New Testament, then, is to be seen not merely as an occasional episode, celebrating petitions that have been answered, but (as is clear from Paul) as the expression of an abiding attitude which is constitutive of the Christian life.

(a) Thanksgiving in the Gospels

It is, then, surprising that Jesus' teaching on prayer, which has so much to say about petition, is so poor on thanksgiving. True Aramaic, the language spoken by Jesus, has (like Hebrew) no special word for 'thanks'. But the Hebrew Bible is rich in thanksgiving, which is expressed in specialized literary forms like the thanksgiving song (*tôdāh*), or through appropriate formulae like 'to bless (*bārak*) the Lord'. Such Jewish turns of phrase do in fact occur in the Synoptic Gospels (Mark 6.41; 8.7; Luke 1.46–55, 64, 68–79; 2.28), together with occasional occurrences of the Greek *eucharistein* (= 'to thank') and its cognates (Mark 8.6; 14.23; Luke 17.16; 18.11). But they are infrequent. What the Synoptic Gospels have to say about thanksgiving is meagre.

The infancy narratives in Luke have two early Christian canticles, typically Jewish songs of thanksgiving, which celebrate key moments in saving history: the birth of the Baptist (Luke 1.68–79) and the conception of Jesus (Luke 1.46–55). All three Synoptics (following Mark) show Jesus pronouncing (as a good Jew would) thanksgiving over food in the two feeding miracles (Mark 6.41; 8.6f.), and at the Last Supper (Mark 14.22f.). Matthew and Luke give us a prayer of thanksgiving recited by Jesus (Matt. 11.25f. = Luke 10.21). And Luke alone has a saying of Jesus on thanksgiving (the only such saying in the Synoptic tradition), in which Jesus complains that of the ten lepers he had healed, only a Samaritan had come back to give him thanks and so find not just healing but salvation (Luke 17.17–19).

We might be inclined to take the description of the institution of the eucharist at the Last Supper of the Lord (Matt. 26.26–29; Mark 14.22–25; Luke 22.17–20) as the most important reference to thanksgiving in the Gospels. For the eucharist, as its name indicates, is for us the great rite of Christian thanksgiving. But it is doubtful whether the eucharist had this significance in the Gospels. There the giving of thanks is not central to the rite, but is merely a customary grace before meals which prepares for the 'breaking of bread' which follows. It is this gesture of oneness and sharing which is central, and serves to designate the eucharist in New Testament times (Acts 2.42, 46; 20.7; I Cor. 10.16). It is not the Gospel texts on the institution of the eucharist, then, nor their foreshadowing in the two accounts of the feeding miracle worked by Jesus (both of which have been edited to conform to the institution narrative),[14] that will teach us what Jesus has to say about thanksgiving. For this we must turn to the prayer of thanksgiving attributed to him in Matthew and in Luke (Matt. 11.25f. = Luke 10.21), and supplement what we learn there by what is said about thanksgiving in the canticles of Luke 1–2, and in the saying on thanksgiving which concludes the Lucan story of the Ten Lepers (Luke 17.17–19).

(b) The thanksgiving prayer of Jesus
   As reconstructed by Siegfried Schulz from its almost identical versions in Matthew and Luke (Matt. 11.25f. = Luke 10.21), the prayer would have read:[15]

> In that same hour Jesus said:
> 'I praise you, Father, Lord of heaven and earth,
> Because you have hidden these things
>   from the wise and understanding,
> And revealed them to babes.
> Yes, Father, for such was your gracious will.'

With its concluding 'Yes, Father . . .', which forms an inclusion with the 'I praise you, Father . . .' of the opening address, the prayer is a rounded unit, complete in itself. It was originally distinct from the revelatory word ('no one knows the Son except the Father') to which it has been attached in Q (Matt. 11.27 = Luke 10.22). In itself and separated from the revelatory word, the Hellenistic vocabulary and explicit christology of which make it unlikely that it was pronounced by Jesus, the prayer of thanksgiving could well be authentic. It is thoroughly Jewish in form; and its content reflects both the attitude of Jesus, with its clear option for the poor, and the situation of his mission, which was successful among the 'little ones' but not among the religious and intellectual elite. The sharpness of the opposition between the 'babes' to whom 'these things' (the presence of eschatological salvation in the words and deeds of Jesus) have been revealed, and the 'wise and understanding' from whom they have been hidden, recalls the uncompromising radicality of so much of the teaching of Jesus which inevitably leads to the separation of conflicting groups. Jesus thus opposes God and mammon (Matt. 6.26), poor and rich (Matt. 6.20–24), tax-collector and Pharisee (Luke 18.9–14), old law and new (Matt. 5.21–48), defilement from outside and defilement from within (Mark 7.15), observance of law and practice of love (Mark 3.1–5). The Q prayer of thanksgiving thus stands well within the specific perspective of Jesus, and may safely be attributed to him.

The prayer begins (as all the prayers of Jesus do) by addressing God as 'Father' (*abba*). The qualification 'Lord of heaven and earth' which follows is (like the addition to the invocation in Matthew's version of the Lord's Prayer) an insertion by the Jewish–Christian community, using a typical rabbinic formula. Yet the insertion is appropriate to the mood of the prayer. For in it Jesus thanks God not for personal favours done to him, but for the form which God's saving action takes in history. The thanksgiving of Jesus is thanksgiving for salvation history!

In this Jesus stands well within the biblical tradition. All through the Hebrew Bible, 'thanksgiving . . . responds to the unique work of God. More or less confusedly, every particular kindness of Yahweh is always felt as one moment of a grand history in the process of realization. Thanksgiving carries biblical history and prolongs it in eschatological hope.'[16] This orientation continues through Jesus into the Christian community. We find it in the canticles of the infancy narratives of Luke, which are good examples of early Jewish–Christian piety. In them, Zechariah gives thanks to God not just for the birth of a son, but because this birth shows that the 'Lord God of Israel . . . has visited and redeemed his people' (Luke 1.68). And Mary's song of thanksgiving, too, which begins by thanking God for the favour done to her (Luke 1.46–49), goes on to thank God for the definitive liberation of his people which this gracious act of God has started (Luke 1.50–55).

The story of the Ten Lepers in Luke (17.11–19) adds a further dimension to this. The Samaritan who returns to thank Jesus is told, 'Rise up and go, your faith has brought you salvation' (Luke 17.19). Thanksgiving is here identified with saving faith! The story, with its double saying of Jesus and its distinctively Lukan vocabulary, has little likelihood of being historical. As it stands it is largely a Lukan composition. But what it says about thanksgiving is fully consonant with the teaching of Jesus. For the point it makes is that, being an expression of faith, thanksgiving (like petition) is a constitutive element of Christian life.

(c) The problem of prayer and action
There is a danger, obviously, that such a life, built on petition and thanksgiving, could lead to passivity and fatalism. Prayer of petition can easily become a substitute for effective action; and thanking God in all things can easily lead to a passive acceptance of unjust situations. But this did not happen to Jesus or to Paul. When Jesus urges us to ask for all things with childlike trust, and when Paul invites us to thank God continually, they are not exhorting us from the security of a cloister, but speaking out of the turmoil of intensely active and conflict-filled lives. If prayer was not for them an excuse for inaction, it is because they understood prayer (petition and thanksgiving) as always related to the Kingdom of God and to its realization in history.

For the Kingdom of God is both a gift and a task. God's love for us is shown precisely in its profound respect for human freedom, and in its challenging summons to humankind to assume responsibility for its history. They love of *abba* is not paternalistic or maternalistic, but a love that fosters responsibility and growth. To pray for the Kingdom means, therefore, to assume responsibility for our part in the personal, communitarian and societal revolution which the Kingdom brings. To thank God for salvation history is to acknowledge the demands which that history makes on us. And, slightly adapting a well-known maxim of Ignatius of Loyola, to pray as if everything depended on God is also to act as if everything depended on ourselves alone.

Notes

1. L. Cerfaux, *Recueil Lucien Cerfaux, Tome III*, Gembloux 1962, 253.
2. J. Herrmann, *TDNT* II, 798 (= *TWNT* II, 797).
3. See M. Dhavamony, 'Hindu Prayer', *Studia Missionalia* 24, 1975, 185–92; K. Mitra, 'Cultic Acts in Hinduism', in W. Strolz and A. Ueda (eds.), *Offenbarung als Heilserfahrung im Christentum und Buddhismus*, Freiburg 1982, 127–44.
4. J. Caba, *La oración de petición. Estudio exegético sobre los evangelios sinópticos y los escritos joaneos*, Analecta Biblica 62, Rome 1974, 310–16.
5. Statistics indicate this. The verbs *aitein* and *deomai*, the two main verbs used for petition in the New Testament, are found (as prayer) about thirty times in the Gospels and fourteen times in Paul. In contrast *eucharistein* (= 'to thank') is found only eleven times in the Gospels, as against twenty-four times in Paul; and the cognate noun *eucharistia* (= 'thanksgiving') is not found in the Gospels at all, though it occurs twelve times in Paul.
6. Of the two other prayers attributed to Jesus in the Synoptic Gospels, Luke 23.34 is textually doubtful. Even if authentic, it would, like Luke 24.46, be a Lukan

composition formulated to make the death of Jesus a paradigm for Christian martyrdom.

7. Even the *Spiritual Exercises* of Ignatius of Loyola, one of the more technical treatises on prayer in the Christian tradition, would appear curiously unfinished to an Indian reader, accustomed to the meticulous instructions on diet, posture, breathing, and methods of concentration that are detailed in Indian texts on meditation.

8. See F. X. D'Sa, *Gott der Dreieine und der All-Ganze. Vorwort zur Begegnung zwischen Christentum und Hinduismus*, Düsseldorf 1987, 79–95, for a comparison between Christian prayer and Indian meditation.

9. The saying on receiving the Kingdom like a child is found in Mark and Luke attached to the story of Jesus blessing little children (Mark 10.13–16 = Luke 18.15–17). This is found immediately before the story of the Rich Young Man in Mark (10.17–22) and in Luke (18.18–23), and immediately after the parable of the Pharisee and the Tax-Collector in Luke (18.9–14). In these Gospels, then, the Pharisee of the parable and the rich man of the story serve as negative illustrations of what it means to be a child. They show how a child does not receive the Kingdom of God.

10. J. Jeremias, *The Prayers of Jesus*, London 1967, 82–107.

11. S. Schulz, *Q: Die Spruchquelle der Evangelisten*, Zürich 1972, 161–2.

12. Caba, *Oracionde peticion* (n. 4), 310–11.

13. M. K. Gandhi, quoted in S. R. Tikekar, *Epigrams from Gandhiji*, Delhi 1971, 124.

14. See A. Heising, *Die Botschaft der Brotvermehrung*, Stuttgarter Bibelstudien 15, Stuttgart 1966, 61–8.

15. Schulz, *Q* (n. 11), 213–14.

16. A. Ridouard and J. Guillet, 'Thanksgiving', in X. Léon-Dufour (ed.), *Dictionary of Biblical Theology*, London ²1973, 599.

Contemporary Challenges to Prayer

Enzo Bianchi

I. The object in question

The difficulties and unease that Christians nowadays are experiencing with prayer are nothing new for believers. Quite apart from the particular obstacles which the various turning points of history have produced for Christian prayer, prayer has always been a problem. It is something simple, but not easy to do; it is by no means self-evident, since it does not correspond to natural human activity and cannot be categorized under the reductionist headings of emotive spontaneity or the esoteric quest for techniques of meditation and contemplation. According to the testimony of the Gospel of Luke, the disciples already felt the need to be taught about prayer by Jesus, and they went to him to ask, 'Lord, teach us to pray as John also taught his disciples' (Luke 11.1). From the teachings in the Gospels on Christian prayer which clearly distinguish it from the much talking of the pagans (Matt. 6.7) or which warn against hypocrisy and religious falsehood (Matt. 6.5), or lay down a series of conditions which must be observed in prayer (Matt. 5.23–24; 6.6; John 14.13; Luke 18.9–13; Matt. 18.19–20; Matt. 6.7–9; Luke 18.1; 21.34–36), to the New Testament paraenesis which, while confirming how urgent and essential prayer is for Christians (cf. I Thess. 5.17–18; Rom. 12.12; Eph. 6.18; Col. 4.2–3; I Tim. 2.1–8), already faces objections and obstacles to prayer arising out of the life of the Christian communities (cf. the problem of the effectiveness or ineffectiveness of petitionary prayer in John 1.5–8; 4.2–3), we can see the image of prayer as a vital necessity for the Christian but also as characterized by difficulties and laborious spiritual effort.

This tension is in reality a constitutive part of prayer as an approach to the Christian mystery. In fact, according to the biblical revelation Christian prayer, which challenges any anthropocentric self-sufficiency, far from being the consequence of the natural human sense of self-transcendence or originating in the innate human 'religious sense', appears as gift, as the human response to the absolute, prior and gratuitous decision of God to enter into relationship with us. It appears as a welcome and a recognition, by hearing in the Word and discerning in the Holy Spirit a presence which is in us before any effort on our part to attend to it, as a decentralizing of our own 'I' in favour of the 'I' of Christ, in a movement of openness to communion with God through Christ in the Holy Spirit, the conclusion and outcome of which is *caritas, agape*, love. This is in fact the goal of Christian prayer and the point at which its authenticity is tested: compared with it all forms of prayer, including the liturgy and the sacraments, remain means, accidents!

Paul sums up Christian prayer very well as a trinitarian event in that passage of Romans 8 which culminates in the affirmation that 'we do not know how to pray as we ought, but the Spirit himself intercedes for us with sighs too deep for words' (Rom. 8.26). From Paul's text it appears that Christian prayer arises out of a confession of powerlessness and ignorance about prayer itself! So before we face some objections which are made to prayer nowadays, we must relocate it in its biblical context. There it appears straight away that prayer is not a quest for God but a response to God, that its forms are accidental and that its aim is love. The traditional definition of prayer as 'raising up the soul to God' (John of Damascus, Thomas Aquinas) seems inadequate not only on the basis of the biblical revelation from which alone inferences can be made, but also with reference to men and women of today who are allergic to the ascending and vertical conceptions disseminated in Christian spirituality.

The biblical God is the living God who does not stand at the end of our reasoning, and is not found in the logic of our concepts, but reveals himself in his actions. It is he who, from Genesis to the Apocalypse, with a free and sovereign initiative, seeks, asks, calls human beings who, confronted with this revelation – which is a true communication by God of himself in history for the salvation and liberation of humankind – reacts in faith by giving thanks (benediction, praise and so on) and making requests (invocations, intercessions and so on), and does so through prayer (seen in its two essential and constitutive elements, whether at a communal or a personal level, as thanksgiving and petition). The response of men and women in prayer thus becomes obedience and is expressed as love towards God and love towards others: prayer is openness to communion with God, and thus to agape. The 'I' which opens itself to God is definitively decentralized in prayer, and the agent is the God who has loved first and who, by showing his love in the acceptance of our prayer, pours it upon the world through us who are made his lovers.

From this perspective Christian prayer is first of all listening to the Word which leads us to welcome the presence of the Trinity: it therefore requires silence, a capacity to struggle against the idolatry of time and manifold temptation, and soberness and perseverance. Christian prayer thus opens the way to authentic biblical contemplation which is a merciful perspective on the world, achieved by receiving the gift of agape.

II. Prayer: eloquent faith

Having tried to focus on what is meant by authentic Christian prayer, I now go on to a second comment. The difficulties encountered by Christian prayer are directly related to the difficulties encountered by faith. Prayer is in fact always *oratio fidei* (*euche tes pisteos*, James 5.15); i.e., prayer is not only offered with faith but derives from faith. Prayer is the expressive capacity of faith and the eloquent mode of faith. In this light it is dramatically significant that nowadays the difficulties are not so much about how to pray as about why to pray, and that we are seeing a kind of eclipse of personal prayer. Reaction against an individualistic spirituality nurtured on devotional prayers and personal piety has led to a renewal and a renewed understanding of liturgical and communal prayer, but this has yet to bear the fruits of the revival of personal Christian prayer which were hoped for by Vatican II when it launched on liturgical reform.

One has the impression that with so many changes in prayer, a large part of the heritage of traditional Christianity has fallen by the wayside. To try to cope with the situation of spiritual disorientation which they discovered, above all in the 1980s, diocesan organizations increasingly offered courses and schools in prayer, but these have proved inadequate. The growing demand among the young and indeed among the less young has been for spiritual fathers, for *startsy* who know how to direct human and spiritual growth by handing down a wisdom and an experience of prayer. Prayer, like faith, has to be brought to birth. The *traditio fidei* has to be accompanied by the *traditio orandi artis*, the tradition or the art of praying. But unfortunately spiritual figures are lacking, and neither spiritual masters nor masters of prayer can be found at a moment's notice.

Furthermore, the marked and sometimes exclusive stress over the last two decades on the communal, collective and liturgical dimension of prayer in the assembly, detached from an analogous effort at catechesis and education in personal prayer, runs the risk of deepening the gulf between prayer and life and producing a new formalism. Such a formalism is already visible in certain ritualistic attitudes of pan-liturgism and pan-sacramentalism. In addition, the increase in articulate objections to prayer (like those made in the 1960s and 1970s) by Christians themselves, along with indifference and unawareness amounting to a lack of perception that prayer is absolutely vital to Christian existence, amounts to a serious challenge to the quality of faith. Only if the proclamation of Jesus the Lord and therefore the call to follow him resounds through the church with the absolute primacy that it demands, in a way of knowledge which leads to love for the Lord (the true Christian gnosis), will prayer be capable of appearing not as one activity among so many that are required of the Christian, nor just as an occasion for a gathering of the community for social and ecclesial aims (prayers for peace and for human rights), but as the dimension in which to live by experimentation, nurturing the relationship with Christ by showing, in an '"I-thou" dialogue and encounter', one's own commitment to and love for the one who is the Lord of our lives.

The dominant imperative over these last years within the church framework of caritative organization, to work for peace, justice, the defence of human rights, in short to do good by supporting and responding to present-day demands and needs, may on the one hand be seen as a salutary and necessary revival of the awareness of the solidarity of Christians with others, shared responsibility, in the light of the gospel. However, on the other hand, the risk in this development is that it may lead to the building up of a church which is active, effective, present where it is needed, but which poses obstacles to the lordship of Christ by putting commitment, works and the observance of commandments before obedient response to the free, creative and absolute call of the Lord. This pastoral tendency in the church can have a very negative effect on prayer, which must remain the place of free encounter with the Lord, and must always also be the personal, daily and persistent prayer of one ready to respond to the word of the Lord who calls without predetermining in advance the nature of either the service or the obedience. So here there is a primacy of faith over works which must be safeguarded absolutely, and without which prayer loses its foundation and its *raison d'être*.

Without personal prayer, how can Christians live out that quality which is truly specific to the Christian and which defines the identity of people who 'love Jesus Christ without seeing him and though not seeing him now believe in him' (I Peter 1.8)?

III. Prayer: asking *and* thanking

Christian prayer moves essentially and completely between the two poles of asking and thanking; it always proves to be capable of requesting, of asking, and always tends to give thanks. Asking and thanking are expressions of the one event of prayer, of the one act which is always a response to the God who has spoken first. In the Christian economy even petitionary prayer is not so much a spontaneous prolongation of human desire as an obedient response to the Lord's command, 'Ask . . . , seek . . . , knock . . .' (Matt. 7.7). The promise of being heard associated with these imperatives, '. . . and it will be given to you, . . . and you will find, and it will be opened to you' (Matt. 7.7), is already the foundation of the intrinsic and unbreakable bond between asking and thanking, between supplication and thanksgiving, attitudes which are always also present in the Psalms (see e.g. Pss. 22; 28; 31; 69). This difficult synthesis, the spiritual working of faith, is required of those who pray by Jesus' admonition in Mark 11.24: 'Whatever you ask in prayer, believe that you receive it, and you will.'

In fact the God of whom one asks and to whom one gives thanks is one and the same. Therefore the fact that nowadays a serious crisis in petitionary prayer is being met with a revival of prayers of thanksgiving is symptomatic of a crisis in faith, of a pathology which attacks the very image of God and human beings, and creates an imbalance in prayer, i.e. in the relationship between the two partners.

We have to recognize, with the faithful attitude and free speech of God's children, that the God who is praised and blessed is the personal God, the God of Abraham, Isaac, Jacob and Jesus Christ, the God of the covenant, the God of the promises, the God who reveals himself concretely and really in history and in life, the creator God and lord of all things, the God 'in whom we live, move and have our being' (Acts 17.28), and that this is 'the one God from whom all things come and through whom we exist' (I Cor. 8.6), 'the Father' (I Cor. 8.6) to whom we can and may turn to ask for 'good things' (Matt. 7.11), 'the holy Spirit' (Luke 11.13) and the one who gives us our 'daily bread' (Matt. 6.11) and 'everything in the name of Christ' (John 14.13; 16.23–24). If we do not, prayer of thanksgiving too risks missing that movement of encounter with God which is a dynamic relationship between two othernesses and a synergy between two freedoms, and withering in a reassuring monologue of self-glorification which is closed in on itself. Moreover, the New Testament does not limit itself to showing the problems of petitionary prayer, but also indicates the self-deception and illusion which can be hidden by prayers of thanksgiving (think of the prayer of the Pharisee in the Temple, Luke 18.11–12).

Christian prayer therefore knows the intrinsic and interior connection between asking and thanking, and vice versa. It is quite certain that the modern world and the process of secularization have brought about a crisis for prayer, and especially for petitionary prayer.

IV. Two radical questions

(a) Prayer and the evils of the world

There is one question which has arisen in this century and which has summarily put all prayer in question. Is it still possible to pray after Auschwitz? It has rightly been replied that it is possible to pray *after* Auschwitz because people prayed *in* Auschwitz; it is possible because Jews and Christians died reciting the *Shema* and calling on 'Our Father'; it is possible because in the inferno of Auschwitz one can trace the story of the holiness of Edith Stein and so many nameless and faceless Jews and Christians. But the Christian who confesses as Lord and Son of God 'Jesus Christ, and him crucified' (I Cor. 2.2) grounds the possibility of prayer above all in the silence of God and the abandonment felt by Jesus, as he called to God from the cross. There the Son, in the silence, abandoned by the Father, maintained his faithfulness by continuing to call on God as 'his God': 'My God, my God, why have you forsaken me?' (Mark 15.34; Matt. 27.46). Christ's prayer in a shameful situation, an infamous death, on the cross which declared him to be a public sinner, cursed by God, excommunicated from religious society and banned from social contacts, in the a-theistic situation of the cross, the situation without God (*choris theou*, Heb. 2.9) of the cross, is the foundation of Christian prayer in the hell of existence.

By crying out in prayer his fidelity to the God who was abandoning him, Jesus achieved a definitive dispossession of himself, a definitive alienation from himself which realized the love of God in him: 'not my will but thine be done'. At that point the communion of will is also a full communion in the passion, and is full compassion. Certainly the experience of devastating evils, of the suffering of little children and innocents, of the storm of violence which has so tragically marked this century and which is now entering the everyday life of every family through the mass media, often provokes the rejection of a God who accepts evil or who even seems to show a malicious face. God seems incapable of coping with the omnipotence of evil or is perhaps indifferent to it: so why pray to a cruel or at least an indifferent God? However, putting the objection in this way means considering prayer as an expression of a human desire which has experienced failure in the hour of tragedy, a desire which, when it is not realized, openly declares 'the death of God'.

Yet the first question that responsible men and women ask when confronted with the human lapse into violence certainly is whether humanity has not died within the human race, and the believer's question is whether human beings have not died to the reality of God. The face of God is revealed, not shaped or forged by human beings, and human beings can choose whether to accept God's coming in epiphany or to hide away from him. Christians even pray in contradictory situations, thus attesting that their God, safeguarded in his otherness, is really the Lord and not the sublimated and omnipotent projection of themselves. They do so because it is only in laborious prayer that there is revealed to them 'the mystery of God' (Ps. 73.16–17), that 'mystery of God' (I Cor. 2.1, according to the reading of many manuscripts) which offers the Christian gnosis, the content of which is 'Jesus Christ and him crucified' (I Cor. 2.2), i.e. the revelation of the face of God in the face of the crucified one. This is the revelation, in a substantial form, of the participation of God in human suffering.

(b) Prayer and secularization

The other major and radical objection to the validity of prayer stems from the process of secularization which has marked the whole of the modern era and in particular the twentieth century. Secularization, essentially characterized by the affirmation of the full autonomy of science and technology from the religious sphere, of the desacralization of the world and life and the heightened sense of human responsibility towards the history of the world, has certainly helped to purge practical Christianity of its remaining magical and ritualistic aspects and has stressed the active role of human responsibility in the planning of our world; it has denounced the image of a God who is too often reduced to a God of the gaps, making up for human deficiencies, a *deus ex machina* who comes to the rescue where their natural limitations prevent human beings from doing so, etc. Under the impact of this phenomenon prayer has become increasingly 'suspect' of evading human history and human responsibility, and in particular has been put in a state of profound crisis, to such a degree that many people now think that petitionary prayer and, more precisely, prayer for God to intervene in temporal matters, is now outdated.

The aspect now presented by the secularized city is that of civilization at an advanced stage of technological development; it is that of a world of science and technology which presents itself as 'methodologically' atheistic, which aims at the rigorous imperative of 'objectivity' and explains events and phenomena on the basis of their interconnections, necessarily eliminating any recourse to the creator God. The radical breach in the covenant between human beings and nature and the immediacy of their relationship, involving human occupation of areas which at one time were exclusively the sphere of the intervention of God, has led to a cultural climate marked by a sense of the increasing distance and insignificance of God, and has deepened the gulf which separates prayer from life, with the result that 'while human beings once found support for their faith and the practice of prayer in their environment, nowadays the world around them is an obstacle against which anyone who wants to safeguard faith and the practice of faith must struggle'.[1]

In this context, to recover the fullness of the sense of prayer and faith it is necessary to understand more deeply at a theological and spiritual level the intrinsic unity between creation and redemption, between the creative level and the redemptive level. In scripture creation is presented as an event of salvation, as a paschal event of passing from darkness to light and from chaos to harmony (Gen. 1), as a transition from non-being to life (Gen. 2), and salvation is always presented as a re-creation (Ezek. 37). Then Christ, 'the firstborn of all creation' (Col. 1.15), the Christ 'in whom, through whom and for whom all things were created' (Col. 1.16–17), is the one who has presided over creation as over redemption; he is the one mediator of the gifts of a covenant which is not only bound up with the economy of redemption but is already expressed in the economy of creation.

That so often petitionary prayer for good things has been regarded as a lower form of prayer, as being too materialistic and self-interested, alien from 'pure prayer' in contrast to the superiority of the request for spiritual goods and thus for salvation, has come about not only as a reaction against a deviant form of prayer reduced to utilitarian requests, but also as a result of a substantial lack of esteem for the level of creation and human realities. This lack of esteem is associated with an attitude which makes a rigid connection between salvation on the spiritual level and an other-worldly level, in the name of a categorical distinction between human and spiritual dependence which derives from a non-biblical, dualistic attitude.

For scripture, then, creation did not take place once for all so that it is shut up in the past, but it is a continual process: it is *creatio continua*. Each instant exists because God is alive, present and at work; each instant is an act of creation. Here lies the great difficulty of discerning the presence of God in reality and his activity in history, an activity which is essential to prayer, above all to prayer of thanksgiving.

We can make a start in replying to this question, which is a pressing one in a technological era, by recalling that according to the biblical revelation, the created world is a world in which human beings are called to intervene. This intervention is a vocation which human beings have received from God to cultivate and guard the earth, to rule and exercise lordship over creation, a lordship which offers human beings the possibility of co-creating with God.

So here is a positive element in technological and scientific development which can even bring blessings (cf. Gen. 1.28; 4.17–22); however, this positive element is threatened by a parallel development: progress of evil and the capacity to do evil. Technological progress, like anything which lies in human hands, remains ambiguous and can bring curses (exploitation, oppression, death). The growth of the human capacity to control reality, as particularly this last period of the twentieth century has shown, has gone hand in hand with the achievement by the human race of the capacity to destroy itself, and moreover this has taken place at the price of an indiscriminate exploitation of the natural environment which has dangerously upset the balance of nature.

Prayer has its context here, not in competition with technology nor with a view to replacing it, but in recalling that technology is in the service of humankind and God's plan, and that it cannot become an instrument of human oppression or be so absolutized that it becomes a new god, an idol. That pledges believers to remain in that area of obedience to the Father and of full responsibility towards their brothers and sisters, human beings ('Our Father . . .'), through which alone their work in the world can be the vehicle of the blessing of the God of the covenant.

With petitionary prayer believers accept in a radical way that God remains God, refuse to see themselves as the source of life, and reject the temptation to raise themselves to the level of God. Believers know that God has radically entrusted them with all things, but they also know that they must be ready every day to receive all things anew, as a gift, from God, thus bearing witness to the way in which he is the Lord of their own lives and of all reality. In a text of the utmost importance for our understanding of the responsibility of believers before the world and before God, Paul writes: 'The world, life, death, the present, the future, all are yours. But you are Christ's and Christ is God's' (I Cor. 3.22–23).

V. Prayer today: objections and difficulties

(a) The suspicion of the uselessness of prayer

The structuring of everyday life and the cultural conditioning of society are inevitably reflected in the Christian's life of faith and prayer. This produces a climate in which prayer is threatened 'from the outside' (the secularization of society, the rhythms of work, the imperative of efficiency and productivity, and so on), and often it is not even encouraged 'from the inside' (the aspects of worldliness increasingly present among Christians, the dismissal of the demanding radicalism of the gospel). The sphere of temporality is the area in which many of the difficulties in praying appear: lack of time, lack of constancy, discontinuity and the inability to persevere, the fading of a sense of eschatology and 'eternal life'. Faced with all this, Christians have to withdraw from the idolatry of our time, from the temptation to allow themselves to be dominated by time, from the alienating ideology of work and productivity, from the dominance of action, from the imperative of haste which calls for 'everything immediately, here and now'. Prayer demands a discipline of time, a sacrifice of some of one's own time and therefore of one's own life, in order to dedicate oneself to listening to the Lord and conversing with him; it is nurtured by waiting and patience, and is effective if it is insistent (Luke 11.8; 18.1–8). It tries to be continuous (Luke 18.1; I Thess. 5.17), i.e. constantly open to the presence of God, and never imposes its own times on God but enters into the times and the sphere of God so as to recognize the dimensions of eternity, of eternal life, of the kingdom as the final hearing of any request, the hearing of the great petition 'Thy kingdom come!'

The distractions which inevitably disturb those who pray can lead to discouragement and the abandonment of prayer; believers will try to integrate them into prayer, to transform them into prayer, thus leading to an increasingly profound unification of themselves in the face of that presence of God which alone brings freedom from distractions and introspection. This aspect of struggle (against distractions and manifold temptations) indicates the laboriousness of prayer and the complexity of the spiritual effort which it requires: nowadays more than ever it is burdensome to remain in silence, solitude and inactivity for some time in the same place, in the expectation of hearing from the scriptures so as to discern a presence which cannot be seen but which examines the feelings and thoughts of the heart (Heb. 4.12), and which calls for self-knowledge and a presentation of one's own situation. Then the objection naturally arises that commitment and work are already themselves prayer. But we need to ask whether all the

activism and the sheerly generous, caritative commitment of many Christians today does not conceal a suspicion of the uselessness of prayer and
mistrust of prayer as an effective element in history.

If God knows everything ('Your heavenly father knows what you need',
Matt. 6.32), if God is immutable in his plans ('in him there is neither
variation nor shadow of change', James 1.17), is it not perhaps useless to
make requests of him? These objections, which are already ancient (Origen,
De oratione V. 6), are now returning, aggravated by a failure to resolve the
relationship between prayer and life at the spiritual level. Without confusing
utility with utilitarianism and uselessness with gratuitousness, we could say
that authentic Christian prayer has some utility, that it produces positive
fruits which are not only spiritual but also human. Petitionary prayer is not a
magic formula for transcending and escaping our limitations; on the
contrary, it is founded on our weakness, and is possible only on the basis of a
recognition of our radical need and poverty. In prayer we become aware of
our limitations and we see that prayer is rooted in our creaturely poverty.
Those who begin to pray by supplicating and asking, asking first of all by
calling upon the Holy Spirit, are in so doing expressing their own lack of
self-sufficiency, confessing that they cannot be saved, recognizing dependence on a presence which is there beforehand and from which they are
ready to receive everything – others, and finally themselves and their own
lives – as a gift coming from him. Here, in the profound human source from
which petitionary prayer springs, we also have the roots of prayer of
thanksgiving, which cannot therefore ever be separated from it. This
elementary recognition of our own limitations is the first step in going on to
find access to the deepest truth about oneself: in human terms it is a salvific
act. That alone is enough to indicate the utility of petitionary prayer. But
here we see how the difficulties encountered by prayer for the most part arise
from the image of humankind currently dominant.

The predominant human paradigm today is *homo technologicus*, the
human being who puts his trust in his own technological know-how to
overcome limits and obstacles which only a short time ago were judged to
be insurmountable, someone who posits himself as the beginning and the
master of the technological apparatus by means of which he relates to the
greater part of reality, in other words someone who is motivated by the
need to discover in all his activities an efficacy which is immediately
quantifiable. The risk in the application of this mentality to the spiritual
field and to prayer in particular is the distortion of prayer itself when set
within a mechanistic vision of 'question and answer' in which it is essential
to be able to programme and quantify the concrete result of prayer.

When transferred to the level of prayer, the established anthropocentrism of scientific and technological culture makes human beings the centre and protagonists in a relationship which in reality has its beginnings in God himself and risks reducing prayer to simple reflection with a view to adjusting one's own psychological equilibrium. Thus what is an authentic gift of grace that can flower in the field of persistent prayer, irrigated by the abundant rain of the effective word of God, becomes the goal which is pursued with one's own efforts, and with the help of the human sciences.

The anthropocentric climate which is present within the church itself, increased human self-awareness, certainly makes problematical the acceptance of the very preliminaries which petitionary prayer involves: awareness of one's own limitations and creaturely poverty, the need for salvation, openness to the Other through a relation with him, the readiness to receive! Petitionary prayer, presenting ourselves to God in poverty and need, is the place in which we agree to engage in dialogue, to enter into relationship with God, not on the basis of our own strength or riches, but on the basis of our poverty and weakness, thus opening ourselves to the possibility of letting ourselves be loved and experiencing the love of God for us. Thus in prayer the weaknesses and the miseries which occur through our lives are transformed and become the precious place of a relationship of love. So here prayer is really useful and effective, at least at a subjective level, i.e. that of the person who prays.

(b) Is prayer an effective component of history?

Is there not in the present-day prayer of many Christians, which is so focussed on praise and thanksgiving to God, a lack of the essential aspect of biblical and Christian prayer as an authentic component of history? Or even the attitude of barely hidden suspicion about the possibility of prayer as acting in synergy with the will of God so as to influence history? And conversely, in the contemporary quest for the miraculous and the supernatural, the rage for appearances and visions, is there not an attempt – clumsy if not degenerate – to express and restore a fundamental article of the biblical and Christian faith which is nowadays set about with hesitations and sceptical reservations: namely faith in the God who really works and manifests himself in history? What are we to say of a *Liturgia Horarum* (*lex orandi – lex credendi*) which deprives Christian prayer of the so-called cursing psalms, the instrument by which the poor and the oppressed denounce their historical ills, asking God to do justice by abstaining from doing justice themselves? These are psalms which, while calling on God to establish divine justice, sanction the principle of nonviolence, pledging the one who prays not to yield to the temptation to render evil for evil. The psalms, and the cursing psalms in particular, here provide the best lesson on how prayer which calls for the aid and intervention of God accompanies human action and commitment in history. Petitionary prayer calls for commitment!

This, then, is the profound significance of petitionary prayer for others, intercession. This full dimension of prayer for others, based on the fact that intercession *par excellence* is the action of the Son who has become flesh to suffer death on the cross, made sin for us, was certainly lost in the centuries of the *devotio moderna* and must again find an adequate and balanced understanding in the years after Vatican II. Intercession, i.e. bearing others up in our prayer, is a matter of taking a step in favour of someone with someone else (*intercedere* = interpose), and brings us into solidarity with the God made man *propter nos homines*. In intercession I recognize my utter limitations in doing good for others and dispose myself to accept the other beyond my capabilities: praying for others is the most evident sign and most mature fruit of our responsibility towards others. This also makes it an obligation which goes beyond the public sphere, in that it is neither required by social conventions nor leads to anything in return, not even personal gratification. Intercessory prayer has as the extreme limit of the assumption of responsibility for others *agape* to the point of death on the cross (cf. John 13.1; Phil. 2.8). The intercession *par excellence* of which the intercession of Christians is a part is that of Christ who stretches out his arms on the cross, calling for forgiveness for those who have crucified him (Luke 23.34). It is thus required to embrace all humanity, making the extreme testimony of one's own death an act of love which shows the power of God to be mercy for all. And in this act the believer recognizes and confesses the utterly effective intercession, total intercession, of Jesus – without limits, bearing salvation for all humankind.

(c) Is petitionary prayer heard?

Unease about intercessory prayer also arises from scepticism about the possibility of prayer being heard. Not that there is any possibility of external, measurable and quantifiable verification of its being heard. People often say, 'I prayed so much, but it didn't make any difference'. This cannot in fact be said by believers, who are always directed from the mystery of prayer to the mystery of faith and so to the mystery of God. The Gospels and the New Testament call on the believer to ask in prayer and say how effective this is (cf. Matt. 7.7; John 5.16, etc.), but also indicate a series of conditions so that it does not remain a monological expression of a claim, but becomes true dialogue within a relationship between two wills, two freedoms, two othernesses.

So prayer is to be made with faith (Mark 11.24), with the humility of the one who is aware of not knowing what is appropriate to ask (Rom. 8.26), in the name of Jesus (John 14.13), in the Holy Spirit (Gal. 4.6), with perseverance (Luke 18.1; 21.34–36), always along with a praxis of reconciliation and forgiveness towards the brethren (Matt. 5.23–24), in the awareness that this opens up a relationship of grace with the Lord. But once this has been said, can just anything be asked in prayer? Modern believers feel a sense of discomfort about prayers which ask for something precise and concrete; this restraint leads them to avoid making precise requests to God as though excusing in advance the fact that these requests will not be heard, and always leaving a way out with generalized and vague formulations. However, this attitude tends to obscure a basic attitude of petitionary prayer, an attitude which constantly recurs also in the structures of supplication in the Old Testament: the presentation of one's own particular situation to the Lord. The psalmist has an insight into his own life; he clearly interprets his own situation of need, and through prayer lays it before God in order to arrive at a way of judging and deciding with God on his own circumstances. The psalmist offers to God his own situation of illness, temptation, mortal danger, calumny and unjust persecution, sin, and so on, and asks God to stretch out his powerful arm, which saves in precisely these situations. Authentic Christian petitionary prayer is not the presentation to God of all our desires and a request for them to be heard; it is first of all a request for God to become related to our and others' weakness. The essential thing is not the object of the request but the space for freedom and free speaking in the Holy Spirit within which the one who prays, i.e. the child, the creature, can address God with the cry 'Abba, Father'.

The prayer of the Psalms, the canonical prayer of the church, thus overflowing with requests for salvation, healing, *shalom*, justice, leads Christians to talk of God by recognizing their own creatureliness and the material nature of their limitations and the needs associated with these limitations. It also leads them, knowing that what 'is written' in the Psalms is fulfilled in Jesus Christ, to recognize that all their requests have been heard,[2] and that the prophetic and spiritual effect of the prayers of the Psalms is effective, has an outcome and leads to a hearing, by making them grow to the stature of Christ, by conforming them, under the guidance of the Holy Spirit, to the Son himself. The efficacy of prayer, the fact that it is heard, is perceived only in the faith of the one who makes the prayer: 'The discovery of the efficacy of prayer is bound up with the progress of our inner life and our faith. Little by little we discover that prayer is our most powerful and most intense act because it is in prayer that we work most with God. And it will be our last action in the hour of our death.'[3]

VI. Prayer through Christ

So believers turn with confidence to the Father and Creator, modelling their own petitionary prayer on that of Christ (cf. Mark 14.35–36) and thus disposing themselves to discern the thoughts of God by accepting the promptings and the requests through which they began to pray, turning their own desires into the desire of the Spirit (Rom. 8.27), integrating the request for 'material gifts' with that of 'spiritual gifts', and always committing their requests to the hierarchy present in the 'Father'.

The petitionary prayer of Christians respects the autonomy of earthly realities and the laws which govern them and also respects and affirms the secret presence of God in this world of science and technology. Without ever claiming to prescribe to God the manner and time of the salvation called for, with petitionary prayer believers try to enter into the plans of God, not to force God to follow their own. Believers know that prayers made in Christ will always be heard by God, who always gives the Holy Spirit, the gift of gifts, to anyone who asks him (Luke 11.13). Indeed, as Bonhoeffer writes, 'God does not give us everything we want, but he does fulfil all his promises, i.e. he remains the Lord of the earth, he preserves his church, constantly renewing our faith and not laying on us more than we can bear, gladdening us with his nearness and help . . . all that we may rightly expect from God, and ask him for, is to be found in Jesus Christ . . . If we are to learn what God promises, and what he fulfils, we must persevere in quiet meditation on the life, sayings, deeds, sufferings and death of Jesus.'[4] And it is in Christ, to whom believers are bound by an eternal covenant which reaches into their personal situation ('he has loved me and has given himself for me', Gal. 2.20), that the promises of God have become 'yes' (II Cor. 1.20).

The believer who, moved by the holy Spirit, prays to God through Christ, with Christ and in Christ, receives from the very prayer of Jesus the revelation of the image of God as 'the Father': Jesus' prayers of thanksgiving (Matt. 11.25; Luke 10.21; John 11.41) and petition (Matt. 26.33; Mark 14.36; Luke 22.42; 23.34; John 12.27; 17.1ff.) are always based on the recognition and the confession of God as 'Father', 'My Father', 'Abba'. Prayer is indissolubly associated with entering into a relationship with God as Father. This poses a great human and spiritual difficulty because it involves the full acceptance of our own history, in our own human fatherhood and motherhood, as a basis for moving to the Fatherhood of God; it is, in substance, the burden of the relationship in the acceptance of the otherness, of the difference, and of the scope of the possible conflict. True Christian prayer delivers us over to the most intimate truth about ourselves, to our own deepest personal identity, leading us to recognize the otherness of the other 'which is realized principally in the relationship of the Father to the one whom he recognizes as being the Son'.[5] In Christ is revealed the face of God the Father and Creator; baptized in Christ, believers are involved in a hope of precedence which is the foundation and motive of their petitionary prayer and thanksgiving.

VII. Conclusion

So the prayer of Christians amounts to entering into free space, into the economy of the gift, so as to perceive that 'all is grace' by having known and experienced the personal love of God for oneself (cf. Gal. 2.20).

Prayer arises out of the love of God in Christ Jesus, poured into our hearts through the Holy Spirit, and prayer leads to love, generates love. One of the reasons that can have caused dissatisfaction with, and abandonment of, personal prayer is perhaps the lack of an emphasis that it is devoted to love, to *caritas*, to *agape*. This is the only criterion for the verification of the authenticity and efficacy of prayer: love for the Lord and for fellow men and women. And this lack of it is perhaps one of the two main reasons for the deepening of the gulf between prayer and life, causing many challenges to prayer itself, and encouraging the quest for more refined and complicated techniques and methods of prayer like zen and yoga. For Christians, prayer remains orientated on the one *telos* of love., It is true and authentic prayer to the degree that in it *agape* is increasigly realized.

Translated by John Bowden

Notes

1. D. Staniloae, 'La preghiera in un mondo secolarizzato', *Servitium* 13, 1981, 34.
2. D. Bonhoeffer, *The Cost of Discipleship*, London 1959, 145.
3. M. Legaut, quoted in A. Seve, *Prier aujourd'hui*, Paris 1988, 95.
4. D. Bonhoeffer, *Letters and Papers from Prison*, London and New York 1971, 387, 391.
5. J. C. Sogne, 'La preghiera come invocazione della presenza invisibile e silenziosa del Padre', *Concilium* 9.8, 1972, 27–8.

Prayer and Conceptions of God

Ulrich Eibach

I. Prayer and the Modern World View

Prayer is the centre of religious life, including Christian life, and petitionary prayer is the form which is practised most frequently. This has always
been the object of criticism. Those theologians who had been influenced
by the concepts of God in Greek metaphysics and who therefore stressed
the immutability of God or the divine will had already sought to guard
against possible misunderstandings of petitionary prayer and the idea of
God that goes with it. The omniscient God does not need us to present
our wishes to him, and he 'will not be moved by human words to do what
he had not willed previously'. God is 'not like a man, that he should
change'.[1] This criticism was intensified in the modern period, just as the
conception of the action of God in this world was put in question
generally, and the world was understood 'god-lessly' as a machine which
ran in a regular way that could be described in causal terms. In this world
God can act only by immutable laws of nature or by the determination of
human reason. The only subject acting freely in this world, and thus its
real lord, is man. Human beings are to be able to act freely in this world
and change it, something which is not permitted to God. On these
presuppositions it no longer makes sense for petitionary prayer to ask for
the intervention of God in nature and history; that is to direct it to the
wrong authority, to a God who transcends the world and is incapable of
intervening in it in a contingent way, instead of to human beings
themselves. Where theology did not escape from these presuppositions,
the theology of prayer was first dominated by the question of the world-
view which conditions the possibility of prayer, and secondly had to make
radical reinterpretations of petitionary prayer, mostly at the same time
moving it into the background in favour of other forms of prayer
(thanksgiving, praise, adoration) which implied less clearly defined con-

ceptions of God and therefore could more easily be reconciled with modern thought.

Thus for Friedrich Schleiermacher (1768–1834) thanksgiving became the centre of prayer. In his view the divine rule of the world is exercised only through the natural laws, so that God is the cause of all that is and at the same time the guarantor of its order and meaningfulness. The metaphysical postulate of the 'immutability' of God recurs in Schleiermacher to the degree that God's action in his creation is bound up with the unchangeable laws of nature. For Schleiermacher religion is the 'feeling of absolute dependence' on God and – as God is the cause and the ground of all that has come into being in nature – also on nature.[2] Since what is cannot be otherwise, on the basis of natural laws willed by God, in the last resort prayer can only be aimed at resignation to destiny, grateful recognition of fate as God's saving dispensation. Because all that is is in any case ordered by God for the best, and there can be no evil in nature, in the last resort, when it comes to his or her fortunes, the Christian has nothing to ask for, and the church has as far as possible to refrain from 'wishing', especially as there can be 'no reciprocal relationship . . . between creator and creature'.[3] If God is the ground and cause of all that is, God's will and the course of the world coincide.

Kant was no less influential in Protestant theology. While for Schleiermacher God is the ground and guarantor of the natural order of the world, for Kant he is the guarantor of the moral order, a cipher for the binding character of the moral law. Prayer therefore amounts to 'nothing but the intention to lead a good life',[4] reflection on innate human moral capabilities and obligations and a stimulus to act accordingly. Thus prayer itself produces its object, moral action. Prayer is reflection on oneself. Petitionary prayer directed to a God who exists outside human beings and hears them is a 'vanity' of which enlightened people should be ashamed, because they are not taking seriously the fact that human beings are the only subjects in this world whose action is intentional. To the degree to which the relationship of God to this world became questionable, the idea of God and with it the theology of prayer and prayer itself underwent a crisis. Prayer lost its relationship to a God who is over against human beings and can be addressed as such, to a God who is a person. This leaves those at prayer by themselves, and prayer becomes reflection on one's own possibilities of action.[5] Whether prayer is really calling on God or only a process within the psyche, a conversation with oneself, is ultimately decided on the basis of whether and how God is different from human beings and the world or whether the concept of God is only used functionally as a cipher for the unconditional nature of moral obligation or for the ground, the depth, the totality and meaningfulness of reality as we find it. The functionalization of the concept of God is matched by the function assigned to prayer, which either has a primarily therapeutic, tranquillizing function (as in Schleiermacher) or is a stimulus to moral action (following Kant). In both cases prayer loses its character as dialogue involving a call on God who is not a function of this world and is primarily called on because he is God.

II. Prayer as a criterion of our talk of God

Christian theology is thoughtful reflection, a conceptual clarification of faith. If prayer is the essential point at which faith is alive, then it is the origin and the norm of Christian doctrine about God, the rule of prayer is the rule of faith, and talk *to* God is the foundation for and criterion of talk *about* God. Indeed, the doctrine of God ultimately cannot express anything more or anything different 'from prayer, even if it says it in a different way'.[6] It is involved in making the language of prayer precise in conceptual terms. Prayer is grounded in the prevenient saving action and word of God (Rom. 10.14). Therefore hearing precedes prayer; indeed men and women need to be taught how to pray properly (Luke 11.1). As Holy Scripture is the primary testimony to the decisive words and actions of God, we have to look in it primarily for instruction about how to pray rightly and for the doctrine of God implied in it. In view of the dilemma which the modern world-view has posed for the doctrine of God and the doctrine of prayer, before we ask about the conditions for the possibility of intellectually 'honest' prayer in the present time we need first to consider the biblical dimensions of prayer, especially petitionary prayer, for although it is disputed, it is central in the Bible.

1. The structure of biblical prayers of lamentation and petition
Petitionary prayer in the Old Testament is derived from prayers of lament.[7] It presupposes another who hears the lament and with whom the plaintiff already had a relationship before experiencing distress, another whom he has called on and praised as his God. The understanding of God underlying these prayers of lament is primarily that of a personal 'guardian God' who can be called on directly from any situation. Whereas previously the one who is affected by distress had experienced God's protection, goodness and blessing and therefore praised him, now in the lament he expresses the fact that so far he has had different experiences of God (Ps.

22.11) and in the salvation history which has been told him has heard differently from what is now befalling him (Ps. 22.4ff.; 77.11). Suffering in distress becomes suffering the hiddenness of the gracious countenance of God (Ps. 22.2; 42.3), indeed being cast out by God (Ps. 77.8; Isa. 38.12). The picture of the powerful 'guardian God' who only protects and blesses shatters under the experience of extreme distress on the part of individuals or the people (as in the exile).

The suppliants of Ps. 88 and Job are the most shattering witnesses to this. Job's real suffering consists in the 'conjunction of his profound knowledge that in what has happened and what has come on him he has to do with God, and his no less profound ignorance how far he has to do with God'.[8] Precisely in venturing to accuse this enigmatic God, Job arrives at the insight that in this God he nevertheless also has his heavenly advocate and redeemer (Job 16.19; 19.25). In this way 'the image of God now splits; alongside the hidden God, by whom Job sees himself pursued as by an enemy, there appears the divine witness and redeemer who brings about Job's justification, who guarantees the acceptance of Job by God – even though his physical existence may have been long since extinguished'.[9] Job is no longer concerned with his prosperity but with the nearness of God in life, in suffering and beyond death. Job is not comforted by an explanation of suffering but by an encounter with the living God himself, which in turn takes place in 'riddles', though these indicate God's concern for all that is (Job 38–41) rather than rescuing the wholeness of the world order attested in wisdom – as represented by Job's friends – from the meaninglessness which Job experiences. The difference between an interpretation of the meaning of suffering and the experience of the living God is indicated in Job when he has to confess that so far he has known God only by 'hearsay', but has now seen him with his eyes (42.5) and in doing so is justified. So the only convincing answer to the experience of suffering is the human encounter with God, the experience that the redeemer lives and that he is also there in suffering (19.26f.; 42.5; cf. Ps. 42.3). Job calls this God out of his hiddenness with his lament, which is intensified to the degree of becoming an accusation. He cannot be the 'mere object of human ideas' (Kant) nor a cipher for the course of the world, the destiny, the totality, order and meaningfulness of all existence; he must be a living God who can emerge from his hiddenness, and thus can answer the cry that reaches him.

In these prayers of lamentation there is an unmistakable distinction between prosperity and the experience of the nearness of God (Ps. 22.20); indeed, at the heart of human distress lies a broken relationship with God and the resultant inability to praise him. So the request for God to turn his face towards the suppliant can take priority over the request to remove the distress (Ps. 63.4; 73.25f.). This is a late development in the history of Israelite piety which presupposes the experience of the shattering of the image of God as a powerful guardian God – not least in the exile. If there is this distinction between the request for God's nearness and the request for the abolition of distress, i.e. also between God and his gifts and on the human side between faith in God and experience of healing, then it must be possible for trust in God also to arise independently of his helping intervention. This comes about through the word of promise, which in contrast to the transitoriness of all earthly things abides 'for ever' (Isa. 40.8; Ps. 119.89). The one who laments therefore experiences God turning to him in grace first of all in his answering word of promise, in which God assures the suppliant who calls on him by his name ('Father', 'our redeemer', Isa. 63.16): I know you by name, you are mine, I am with you, I keep my promise (Isa. 41.10, 14: 43.1 etc.).

Petitionary prayer has the character of dialogue more clearly than prayer of praise and thanksgiving; it has the structure of a call and an answer which is sought. If we understand the relationship of God to the world and that of human beings to God in terms of petitionary prayer, it is not to be thought of in terms of an ontology of substance, as an essential bond between two substances of the same nature. Rather, in prayer God is believed in as the free Lord of creation and history and as one who stands personally over against human beings, who has resolved to be there with his creatures and who turns to these creatures in freedom. So God is not subject to the causal pattern of this world. The causal concept to be found in an ontology of substance (cause and effect) is no use for characterizing relationships through which a community of independent (free) persons is built up in talk together and in common action, in which the one 'promises' the other love and faithfulness without being ontologically dependent on the other. Prayer brings out such a 'relational ontology', takes place on this basis, and is therefore to be kept completely free from the concept of 'causality' derived from the ontology of substance and thus from the notion that petitionary prayer could be the cause which necessarily has the effect of an answer from God. The 'reciprocal influence' between God and human beings which comes about in prayer is not to be understood as an ontological influence but as a 'conversation',[10] as a call and an answer (Ps. 51.15), in which the call (lament, petition) is grounded in the preceding word of God's promise (the promise of the covenant) (Rom. 10.14ff.). God's answer consists in his assurance of the renewal of this promise. Whereas in praise and thanksgiving God is still worshipped as the unchangeable and nameless ground of all being and his action can follow the course of the world, this is inconceivable in prayers of lament and petition, since the one who prays experiences the distress he or she receives from the course of the world as a contradiction to the promise given by God.

2. Prayer and the mutability of God

Those who pray, contrast the sorry reality they experience with the God in whom they believe and thus ask whether and how God is related to this reality. This question is clarified not in reflection and talk about God but in address to God, indeed in accusations against him, in the human struggle with God in which God is challenged to provide an answer. As those who pray cannot reconcile their fate with the promised goodness of God, they must assume that God's action towards them must have consciously changed, so that their fate is a punishment from God. They count on God's 'repenting' of his punishment on the basis of their prayer, or at least on his emerging from his concealment. God must therefore be capable of entering into the changing reality of life and of altering his behaviour accordingly.[11] This need not necessarily mean that God again proves to be the old 'guardian God' who restores the old whole order of life, but means that God shows that he is present even in the changed situation, how he is present and remains faithful to those who pray.

Prayer itself takes on decisive significance for the clarification of this question, for in the 'conversation' between human beings and God, those who pray experience the approach of God to their fate. As a result the impossibility of reconciling God's nearness and the experience of distress becomes less, and the experience of God's nearness no longer depends primarily on the removal of distress.[12] The person who prays now experiences that God gives his Holy Spirit (Ps. 51.13) and with it the certainty that neither death nor life can cause separation from God (Ps. 73.26; 139.7ff.; Rom. 8.38f.; 14.8). The distress which leads to the danger of isolation from God (and also from human beings) is thus primarily overcome at this central point, the experience of remoteness from God. In prayer the person who prays receives the gift of the Holy Spirit and thus the assurance of being heard by God and the nearness of God. The prayer for help born out of need is then heard, and trust in God is restored, although not all the content of the prayer has yet been fulfilled. In the prayer the person who prays experiences that God is neither the 'old' guardian God who simply averts distress, nor indeed an unchangeable God who transcends the world, who is the cause and guarantor of the order and meaningfulness of reality as it is.

A God who is thought of as the cause of the evil that destroys my life can hardly be identified with a gracious God on whom the creature can call by name; at all events he has to be seen as an inexorable, unalterable 'law of the world', which simply compels a surrender to destiny. A God who is unaffected by the suffering of his creatures and is incapable of suffering will not have mercy upon them, and in the last resort cannot be near to them in suffering. Thus in Israel, under the experiences of distress in the exile, the conception of Yahweh as the powerful guardian God changed into a God who is affected by the suffering of his people (Hos. 11.8; Heb. 4.15), indeed who draws the evil in this world upon himself and overcomes it in his suffering (Isa. 53) by first removing its 'sting' (I Cor. 15.5), namely the possibility that it separates from God. So the 'suffering servant of God' points beyond the death of Jesus Christ on the cross, in which God came closest to suffering humankind and out of love overcame the heart of evil not through his power but through his suffering. So suffering becomes not only the place where faith is assailed by the hiddenness of God, but at the same time the place to which God is especially near and where he is especially present (cf. II Cor. 12.9). The changeability of God which is presupposed in petitionary prayer is thus made more precise and at the same time deeper as a result of these changes in the image of God which came to birth in the distress of the exile. For God to change does not mean that he becomes another, or even that he gives himself up, but that he descends and enters into the distress and depth of human existence.

Israel got as far as this knowledge of God by contrasting in prayer the distress of the exile with God and his promises. Prayer could be the place at which such knowledge of God also comes about in the life of the individual. Conceptions of God taken over from 'hearsay' (Job 42.5) can be both a help and a hindrance to prayer.

In the New Testament the 'God of the Old Testament' loses his remoteness and also his threatening two-faced character as a gracious and merciful God on the one hand and an enigmatic and punitive God on the other. God comes so near to human beings that they are to address him as 'Father'. God's graciousness and his saving will become his manifest 'countenance'. That leaves the right to lament to God (Matt. 27.46; Mark 15.34; Heb. 5.7; Rom. 8.23), but not in the sharp form of the accusation. A God who himself shares in the suffering of his creation can hardly be accused. However, the suppression also of the lament in church history is a consequence of the acceptance in theology of the metaphysical concept of God and the Stoic image of humanity. The lament disappeared from prayer the more God came to be conceived of as the unmovable mover, raised up above the changes in this world, as the 'apathic' God who is not affected by suffering, and as the guarantor of order and meaningfulness in the world as it is. The experience of distress then calls for interpretations of the meaning of evil and suffering and thus for a transcending, through acts of thought, of the contradiction which we experience and live through between the misery of the world and the goodness and meaningfulness that is claimed for it. These acts of thought lead either to a theodicy and cosmodicy or to atheism or nihilism. To the degree to which God disappears from thought as one who stands personally over against human beings and is displaced by the God of Greek metaphysics, direct address to God is replaced by talk about God as the one who guarantees the meaningfulness of reality. Conversation with God and prayer are now replaced by the thinking of 'theologians' who give a theoretical demonstration of the meaning of all existence, using the concept of God, and thus are meant to provide relief to the uncertainty which emerges as a result of distress.

3. Asking for the giver and asking for gifts – prayer and God's 'omnipotence'

Prayer for God's nearness and communion certainly presupposes the distinction between God and his gifts, but in so doing it does not sever God from his creation and thus his gifts (Luke 11.5ff.). This becomes possible only when the relationship between God and human beings no longer relates to bodily existence but only to the soul, because the soul is supposed to be of divine origin and nature and bears within itself the longing to be reunited with God. According to the Neoplatonic ontology of substance the ultimate concern is not with a relationship between God and creature but a fusion between God and the soul, which are to be of one essence. Only where there is no longer a clear distinction between creator and creature does the distinction between God and his gifts become superfluous. If we are to seek only God himself and not his gifts (Augustine),[13] then this quest ultimately ends up in an essential fusion of God and the soul, and prayer is robbed of its character as dialogue and replaced by meditation, by the sinking of the soul into God and the union of the soul with God, who is imagined as the tranquil and unchanging ground of being. In this way the soul is removed from the painful reality of being human.

Conversely, the danger of 'praying for something' is that one wants the gifts without the giver, that God is ultimately understood only in a functional way, as a cipher for what human beings need unconditionally or desire most ardently. In that case, too, prayer is no longer related to another over against the one who prays, and while the human wish is taken seriously, God is not. The result is a loss, first, of any criteria for a distinction between human wishes and God's will and, secondly, of the character of prayer as a relationship, a 'conversation'. It is no longer grounded in the prevenient word of God, but only in human wishes. In such 'asking', human beings are ultimately left to themselves and they conclude that their wishes will not be fulfilled, that prayer is no use or even that God does not exist. This use of prayer as a means to selfish ends cannot be avoided either by referring those who pray to a God who can give nothing other than the certainty that he is, or with the remark that it is unnecessary to ask God for gifts for this life, as these gifts have already all been ordered for the best in the natural course of the world (Matt. 6.25ff.). In both instances prayer would end up with human beings being content with their painful earthly fate. But that would be to fail to understand the depths of the suffering of creation (Rom. 8.23), in which those who suffer can not only experience the collapse of body and soul but can also be cast into the deepest despair about God. In the lament, those who pray indicate that there is such a contradiction between the reality they find so painful and God's promises that God cannot be believed in as the author of both, and thus who God in fact is, and what are his true being and real will, remains an enigma. In his actions towards human beings God is to demonstrate who he is (Ex. 3.14), and what really corresponds to his will: the experience of suffering or the promise of salvation. In that case at least the prayer for God does not replace the request for his gifts, if human need is so great that men and women no longer see God's face nor experience his goodness (Ps. 86.5, 13, 15, 17; Matt. 7.7ff.), and indeed experience God as an enemy (Ps. 88; Job).

However, if after the final revelation of the saving will of God in Jesus Christ there can no longer be any doubt in the fundamental goodness of God, no conclusions may be drawn from this goodness of God to the thoroughgoing goodness and meaning of the whole world as it is. Such an incorporation of suffering into God's plan with his creation, which makes the suffering of creation innocuous, is alien to the Bible.[14] That those who pray experience the nearness of God as they pray, without their distress being removed, does not mean that God does not want to remove it or that it is willed or even caused by him. For anyone who prays, that raises the question why the healing of the relationship with God is not followed by the healing of the distress (Ps. 103.3; Mark 2.1ff.). Does God not have the power to conquer the evil that destroys his creation? Or does God's descending into the suffering of this wicked world mean that all suffering is participation in the suffering of Christ (II Cor. 4.8), that evil is conquered only by suffering and not by power, that the Christian should therefore be content with faith in this world, because God and his power are present precisely in suffering (II Cor. 12.9)?

Problematic though the conception of the almighty guardian God may be from a theological perspective, it is a no less dubious procedure to misunderstand the suffering God as a helpless God and to exchange traditional talk of the omnipotent God for that of the helplessness of God in this world. In that case God could not be the 'God of all consolation' (II Cor. 1.3), in whom those who pray can set their trust (II Cor. 1.9). Talk of the hiddenness of the power of God in terms of its opposite, the suffering God, only makes sense for Christians if it is incorporated into and subordinated to faith in the power of God who raises the dead (Rom. 4.16; I Cor. 15) and the superiority of God over the powers of evil.[15]

In Israel, in the distress of the exile not only Israel's image of God but also its hope changed. The prophets' message of the new covenant (Jer. 31.31ff.), the new exodus (Isa. 40.3ff.), the new Jerusalem (Isa. 40ff.), the new creation (Isa. 55.6ff.; 65.17ff.) and the all-encompassing kingdom of Yahweh (Dan. 2.44; 7.27; Zech. 14.9) has clearly eschatological features. It does not amount to the restoration of the old, but transcends the old in an all-embracing salvation which clearly has 'transcendental' features, in which all is subjected to God, all evil is excluded: God will be king and reign for ever (Dan. 2.44). The painful reality of the people conflicts with the promises of the 'old covenant'. The prophets renew and transcend these promises at the same time, for a kingdom which embraces the whole world, in which God will first enter on his kingly rule with power and in so doing will show himself as the ruler of all this world. God's all-prevailing power, his omnipotence, is therefore an eschatological predicate. His all-encompassing rule is still in the making.

According to the New Testament view, also, God has still to enter upon his reign (Rev. 19.16; Matt. 6.10); in this world, powers still fight against his rule so that he is not yet 'all in all' (I Cor. 15.25; Heb. 2.8; 10.13). The statements which now already promise God or Christ 'all power in heaven and on earth' (Matt. 28.18) are made within the context of doxologies which look to the rule of God in 'heaven', see the future all-embracing rule of God on earth anticipated in them, and therefore now already praise God or Christ as the 'ruler of all'.[16] In worship of God the hope for the future victory of God over all evil is expressed, and God is now already praised as the one who he will only be by virtue of his power over death, already demonstrated in the resurrection of Christ (I Cor. 15.26, 55). Only when talk of the rule of God was detached from this association with prayer in which God's rule in heaven is praised and at the same time hoped for and called for on earth (Matt. 6.10; I Cor. 15.22; Rev. 22.20), was it stripped of its eschatological dimension, and the future establishment of God's power was replaced by the timeless idea of God's omnipotence, and by the adoption of the philosophical concept of God: the worship of the heavenly and future earthly ruler was turned into the idea of the *deus omnipotens* whose action is either identical with the course of the world (the universal cause) or is arbitrary. This gave rise to the extremely acute problem of theodicy, which is also a burden on prayer. It is a problem for talk *about* God and prayer which has detached itself from Jesus' proclamation of the kingdom of God and from his teaching on prayer, and therefore neither prays to God as 'Father' nor asks for the coming of his kingdom.

All God's promises are summed up in the promise of his kingdom. God's all-embracing goodness is realized with the dawn of the kingdom of God, the renewal and consummation of his creation, which at the same time is confirmation and proof of those earthly goods which correspond to God's will. So the dawn of the kingdom of God is the victorious establishment of God's will, his rule over all creation, the consummation of his life-creating power which has already irrupted upon the powers of evil in the resurrection of Jesus Christ from the dead. So the kingdom of God is the conquest of all those powers which are contrary to God and his will, which destroy his creation. His 'omnipotence' which has become visible in the resurrection of Jesus Christ from the dead is his superiority to the powers of death (I Cor. 15.55, 57; II Tim. 1.10), so that there is no longer any doubt that Jesus is 'Victor' and that the kingdom will one day belong to him (I Cor. 15.24ff.; Rev. 21.3).

4. Prayer for the coming of the kingdom of God and asking for healing

While human beings experience with all other creatures the destructive power of evil in their bodies, at the same time they are the only living beings who know of the promise of the kingdom of God and are therefore caught in the tension of the contradiction between the painful reality that they experience and the fulfilment of the promise of the kingdom of God which is still to come. The lament, the cry for the redemption of the body (Rom. 8.18ff.; Rev. 21.3ff.), is born of this tension. Therefore prayer, lamentation, petition and intercession, and the worship of God which anticipates his eschatological rule, is the way in which hope for the kingdom of God stays alive and proves itself in patient toleration of the tension between the distress that is experienced, the promise that is believed in and the fulfilment that is hoped for (Rom. 5.1ff.). So prayer is the 'praxis of hope', not only the hope of the individual for liberation from distress, but the hope that God will come (I Cor. 15.22; Rev. 22.20) and his kingdom with him (Matt. 6.10), and that as a result the whole creation will be redeemed (Rom. 8.18ff.; Rev. 21.3f.). All asking and intercession, including asking for personal healing, is ultimately aimed at the coming of the kingdom of God into which human individuality is incorporated without being submerged by it, the coming which brings healing with it. In prayer for the coming of the kingdom of God, God's will and human wishes come to be in harmony, because human wishes can be related to the divine promises (Matt. 6.33). This takes place in prayer (Matt. 26.39). Here the person who prays is at the same time brought to realize that these promises apply to all creation, and eyes and heart become open to the sighing of the rest of creation, and the heart is prepared for intercession. The prayer for the coming of the kingdom of God leads to intercession and to the recognition that the individual cannot really be made whole without the redemption of all creation. Therefore in prayer my fate, like that of the rest of suffering creation, is seen against the all-embracing horizon of eschatological hope for the whole of creation.

Now one could say that in this way any prayer in the name of Jesus (John 14.13f.) is heard and one day will also be fulfilled in the coming of the kingdom of God, but that the individual is submerged within a universal horizon of redemption and that moreover the fulfilment of the request is postponed to the eschaton, the last day; so human beings, thus comforted by prayer, and with their specific earthly needs, are again summoned to pious submission to fate. This could be avoided if 'kingdom of God' were understood in Kant's sense as just another term for the moral order of the world, and prayer accordingly served only to quicken the moral disposition in human beings. But Jesus' message of the kingdom of God is a contradiction not only of the moral distress in this world but also of its physical distress. Since modern thought begins from the presupposition that God acts in this world only through the causality of natural laws and the determination of human self-consciousness, the kingdom of God has either to develop through the process of natural law or to be brought about by human action. In this way the conception of the kingdom of God is detached from God's action and becomes a utopia which can be brought about by human beings, towards which men and women direct their actions. In that case there is no longer need for prayer to distinguish correctly between God's will and human wishes, between God's action and human action, between goals which are reserved for God's actions and limited human possibilities. Without prayer, men and women concentrate one-sidedly on their possibilities for action, and neglect to pause in their action, to set themselves before God's face and consider God's action. Prayer is the healthy interruption of human action with a view to God's action.

The postulates of modern thought mentioned above may not become the criteria for proper prayer, which must be governed by God's promise for this world. The resurrection of Christ is the dawn of the rule of God in this world and the anticipation of the new creation in the old (I Cor. 15.26). In the New Testament sickness is understood as the expression of a power hostile to God which destroys life. Jesus' healing of the sick must therefore be understood in terms of God's power of resurrection as a sign of the dawn of God's rule.[17] If the coming of the kingdom of God is the criterion for all prayer for healing, then all prayer for individual healing asks for the symbolic breakthrough and anticipation of the kingdom of God in this life. So in worship God is now already praised as the one who he will only be one day, and human beings may ask not only for the coming of the future, universal, final rule but also for the anticipation of the promised universal kingdom of God in specific individual and social life, even if this always remains sporadic, fragmentary and transitory under the conditions of this age.[18] Calling on God for healing in intercession can therefore be understood – in anthropomorphic terms and not as a causal influence, but on the basis of an 'ontology of relationship' as a 'conversation' between persons – in terms of summoning God to fight against specific evil, 'spurring him on', so that God hears the distress of his creatures and is reminded of his promises which contradict that distress. Such asking is not a matter of God being able to, and doing, what in terms of the abstract notion of omnipotence in nominalism is 'impossible', and doing it above all for me, but of his giving a sign of his goodness which the individual can experience (Ps. 86.17).

The question whether such an intervention of God in the course of history is possible, how and with what means God is doing it, is secondary for the person who prays. Healing brought about by human action which can be explained in terms of natural laws can just as much be a sign of God's activity and an anticipation of the kingdom of God as can unexplained miraculous healing. God's 'omnipotence' is the concrete power to make his promises action and reality, actually in the specific reality of earthly life, without tying himself to means. The question how a God conceived of as the ground of being, who is not one cause alongside others (*causa prima*), can act at the specific level of categories (*causae secundae*) and be experienced in his action, how the 'infinite' can be grasped in the finite, is an important question for fundamental theology, but it may not become the criterion for true praying in 'the name of Jesus Christ'. Petitionary prayer is always justified against the background of the eschatological conception of God's omnipotence, and is also to be encouraged in pastoral care. All prayer in the name of Jesus is a fight for God and for the human cause at the same time; it is a fight for God's rule over the world. To this extent, in prayer, human beings participate in God's rule and government of the world,[19] but prayer is the place where God's will and human wishes manage to coincide (Matt. 26.39). Prayer that relates to God's promises is at the same time the first place where human beings resist evil, resist that human lack of expectation which is content with the facts, and indeed content even with evil.[20] In prayer the *de facto* power of evil in this world is perceived; the person who prays complains about it to God and challenges the right of evil to a place in God's creation with reference to God's decisive action in the death and resurrection of Jesus Christ. Therefore prayer does not encourage quietism, but is rather a challenge to allow oneself to be involved in God's fight against evil with limited human possibilities and in this way to make fragmentary references to the kingdom of God through one's own action. As human beings cannot bring this about through their action, the contradiction between the disaster which is experienced and the salvation which is promised must continually be sustained in prayer. So in prayer human beings take part in the hiddenness of the rule of God in this world, but in prayer they experience the hidden God as the God who is also near, indeed is particularly near, in suffering (II Cor. 12.9ff.).

Translated by John Bowden

Notes

1. Thomas Aquinas, *Compendium Theologiae*, Part II, ch. 2; cf. *Summa Theologiae* II, II q 83 art. 2.
2. F. D. E. Schleiermacher, *The Christian Faith*, Edinburgh 1928, §4, §46.2, §50f., §76.1, §82.2.
3. Ibid., §147.2; cf. §146.1.
4. I. Kant, *Religion within the Limits of Reason Alone*, reissued New York 1960, Part IV, 182f.
5. Thus in W. Bernet, *Das Gebet*, Stuttgart 1970, esp. 87f.; D. Sölle, 'Das entprivatisierte Gebet', in ead., *Das Recht ein anderer zu werden*, Neuwied/Berlin 1971, esp. 135f.

6. G. Sauter, 'Das Gebet als Wurzel des Redens von Gott', *Glauben und Lernen* 1, 1986, 31; cf. K. Federer, 'Lex orandi – lex credendi', *LThK* VI, Freiburg ²1961, 1001f.; G. Ebeling, *Dogmatik christlichen Glaubens* I, Tübingen 1979, 192ff.

7. For what follows cf. C. Westermann, *Lob und Klage in den Psalmen*, Göttingen 1977; E. Gerstenberger, *Der bittende Mensch*, Neukirchen-Vluyn 1980; H. Graf von Reventlow, *Gebet im Alten Testament*, Stuttgart and Berlin 1986.

8. Karl Barth, *Church Dogmatics*, IV.3.1, Edinburgh 1961, 401.

9. H. Gese, 'Die Frage nach dem Lebenssinn', *Zeitschrift für Theologie und Kirche* 79, 1982, 169.

10. Cf. O. Bayer, 'Erhörte Klage', *Neue Zeitschrift für Systematische Theologie* 25, 1983, 262ff.; Ebeling, *Dogmatik* (n.6), 215ff.

11. Cf. J. Jeremias, *Die Reue Gottes*, Neukirchen-Vluyn 1975, esp. 119f., 122f.

12. O. Fuchs, *Die Klage als Gebet*, Munich 1982, 154f., cf. 314.

13. 'God hearkens to your call when you seek him. He does not hear you when you seek something else through him' (*Enarrationes in psalmos* 76.2, PL 36, 971).

14. Cf. E. Gerstenberger and W. Schrage, *Leiden*, Stuttgart 1977; K. Seybold and U. Müller, *Krankheit*, Stuttgart 1978.

15. Cf. U. Eibach, 'Die Sprache leidender Menschen und der Wandel des Gottesbildes', *Theologische Zeitschrift* 40, 1984, 53ff.

16. Cf. E. Schlink, *Ökumenische Dogmatik*, Göttingen 1983, 725ff.

17. Cf. W. Schrage, 'Heil und Heilung im Neuen Testament', *Evangelische Theologie* 46, 1986, 197ff.; W. Bittner, *Heilung – Zeichen der Herrschaft Gottes*, Neukirchen-Vluyn 1984.

18. Cf. G. Greshake, *Grundlagen der Theologie des Bittgebets*; id. and G. Lohfink (eds.), *Bittgebet – Testfall des Glaubens*, Mainz 1978, esp. 68.

19. Cf., H.-J. Kraus, *Systematische Theologie im Kontext biblischer Geschichte und Eschatologie*, Neukirchen-Vluyn 1983, 290ff., 463ff.

20. Cf. J. B. Metz and Karl Rahner, *Ermutigung zum Gebet*, Freiburg 1977, esp. 38f.

Is There Prayer in the Eucharist?

Joan Llopis

An expanded version of the question in the title would be: 'Do people really pray at our eucharists, and do our celebrations encourage people to pray?' A general answer is impossible, because so much depends on particular circumstances. What we can discuss in general terms, however, is whether or not the objective structure of the eucharistic celebration as it has crystallized in the post-conciliar period encourages meaningful prayer among Christians who regularly attend mass.

A general answer to the question would require an analysis of each and every one of the elements of the eucharistic celebration, since all of them – each in its own way – are potential moments of prayer. However, it is perhaps more interesting to limit the discussion to that part of the celebration which is directly intended to get the faithful to pray: the so-called 'Prayer of the Faithful', also known as the 'common' or 'universal' prayer.

Looking at this part of the eucharistic celebration has the advantage of helping us to find out how far the liturgical reforms of the Second Vatican Council have contributed to improving the quality of Christians' prayer lives. Since the prayer of the faithful is one of the most obvious 'novelties' of the post-conciliar mass, its impact on the faithful, whether positive or negative, makes it a criterion of the scope and value of the renewal of liturgical devotion stimulated by Vatican II.

Moreover, since the universal prayer, or prayer of the faithful, is a typical prayer of petition and intercession, reflection on the way it is normally practised by the faithful is very useful as a way of discovering whether or not we Christians 'know how to pray' (Rom. 8.28). In other words, it helps us to discover whether we know how to pray at all, since the most obvious and direct meaning of the word 'prayer' has always been to ask favours of the deity.

We shall therefore centre our reflections on the analysis of the influence of the prayer of the faithful in the mass on the effective practice of petitionary prayer by Christians who take part in it. Our discussion will have the following sections; 1. What is the prayer of the faithful? 2. How does it reflect true Christian petitionary prayer? 3. Does its regular practice teach the faithful to combine prayer and commitment? 4. Suggestions for its revitalization.

I. What is the prayer of the faithful?

The identity and function of universal prayer or prayer of the faithful are very well defined in the description of this prayer in the *Institutio Generalis Missalis Romani* (nos. 45–47).

> In the Universal Prayer or Prayer of the Faithful the people, exercising their priestly office, pray for all. It is appropriate that a prayer of this sort should normally be said at public masses, so that intercessions may be made for the holy Church, for those in public office, for those suffering from various forms of distress and for all people and for the salvation of the whole world.
>
> The order of these intentions shall normally be: (*a*) for the needs of the Church; (*b*) for those who govern the state and for the salvation of the world; (*c*) for those labouring under particular difficulties; (*d*) for the local community. Nevertheless, in some particular celebration, such as confirmation, matrimony or funerals, the order of the intentions may be adapted more closely to the particular occasion.
>
> It is the role of the celebrant to lead these intercessions, invite the faithful to prayer with a brief exhortation, and end the prayers. It is appropriate for a deacon, a cantor or another person to read the intentions, but the whole assembly expresses its intercessions either with a common invocation, spoken after each intention, or with prayer in silence.

The restoration of the prayer of the faithful, decreed by the Second Vatican Council in paragraph 53 of its Constitution on the Liturgy, was an attempt to return to a very ancient tradition. This type of prayer may have Jewish roots, and seems to be apostolic in origin, to judge from I Timothy, referred to by the council's text:

> I urge, then, first of all that petitions, prayers, intercessions and thanksgiving should be offered for everyone, for kings and others in

authority, so that we may be able to live peaceful and quiet lives with all devotion and propriety. To do this is right, and acceptable to God our Saviour: he wants everyone to be saved and reach full knowledge of the truth (I Tim. 2.1–4).

The first clear mention of the universal prayer as part of the liturgical celebration is found in Justin's First Apology. Justin, writing in the middle of the second century, says, with reference to the Sunday eucharist:

When the reader finishes, the president speaks and makes an exhortation or invitation for us to imitate these beautiful examples. We then all stand and make our prayers (67).

And with reference to baptisms, Justin says:

After baptism we bring the person who has believed and has joined us to those who are called the brethren, in the place where they are gathered, to make fervent prayers in common for ourselves, for the person who has just been enlightened and for all others scattered around the world, asking that it may be granted to us, who have discovered the truth, to be found by our deeds to be people of good life and keepers of the commandments, so that we may obtain eternal salvation (65).

Note that Justin always distinguishes these 'common prayers' from the great 'eucharistic prayer', which is pronounced by the celebrant over the bread and wine after the kiss of peace, and to which the whole congregation replies with its solemn 'Amen'.

Hippolytus of Rome, at the beginning of the third century, in his *Apostolic Tradition* (21) prescribed that after baptism the neophytes may 'now pray together with the whole congregation', something which, he notes, they cannot do before being baptized. After the prayer come the kiss of peace and the offering of the bread and wine.

I make no claim to offer a complete account of the historical development of the universal prayer,[1] but it is important to note that there are frequent references to it in many of the Fathers (in the West Cyprian, Tertullian, Ambrose, Augustine, Siricius; in the East Clement of Alexandria, Origen, Athanasius, Chrysostom), though it is not always clear whether they are referring to the prayers said during the celebration of the eucharist.

It is also useful to recall that the solemn prayers which end the Good Friday liturgy of the word are the most ancient texts of the universal prayer in the Roman rite which have come down to us. Baumstark and Jungmann date them to the third century, and they were certainly used very frequently, though later their use was limited to Good Friday. At present the petitions in this solemn prayer are summed up in ten intentions: for the holy church, for the Pope, for all ministries and for the faithful, for catechumens, for the unity of Christians, for the Jewish people, for those who do not believe in Christ, for those who do not believe in God, for those who hold civil office, and for those in distress.

In order to get a clear idea of the essence of the prayer of the faithful as restored by the post-conciliar liturgical reform, it is useful to quote some remarks written some years ago by the liturgist P. Tena, the present sub-secretary of the Congregation for the Sacraments and Divine Worship:

> The name 'Prayer of the Faithful' has caused some misunderstanding. Is the point to ensure that there is a moment in the mass at which the faithful pray? If we put the question in this way, the incoherence of this interpretation becomes obvious. No, the Prayer of the Faithful is not simply the moment in the celebration in which those assembled – the Christian faithful – make their prayers. The 'Prayer of the Faithful' is an element of the celebration with its own well-defined characteristics, as well-defined as, for example, those of the liturgy of the word or of the eucharistic prayer. The 'Prayer of the Faithful' must not be confused with prayer in general; it has its own identity. It is not a moment of meditative prayer in which each person makes his or her own particular legitimate prayers, and then immediately says them aloud. It is not a prayer of thanksgiving like the eucharistic prayer, nor a prayer for offering up works, like the morning prayers of the office. The 'Prayer of the Faithful' is a precisely defined element of the liturgy, a ritual, the paradigm of what the Christian community – the church – should do when it realises that it intercedes, in the midst of the world, with Christ to the Father for human beings.[2]

II. The prayer of the faithful, paradigm of Christian petitionary prayer

It is clear that the prayer of the faithful is a pre-eminent expression of the church's attitude at prayer in its aspect of petition and intercession. Accordingly, it should adequately reflect, in its form and content, the specific characteristics of Christian petition.

For a Christian, the necessity of petitionary prayer does not lie on the level of mere natural religion,[3] as a sort of more or less magic attempt to twist the deity's arm and make him do our bidding. For the Christian, prayer in all its forms, while never ceasing to be a typically religious attitude, is above all an expression of faith. We know that Christian faith is not just one more religion, but we also know that it cannot do without religious forms. And, among all religious forms, prayer is the most immediately suitable to express the personal relationship with God which is the essence of faith.

Religious prayer is a very appropriate instrument for expressing Christian faith, for two main reasons: because it is a typically human mode of expression and because of its ability to display the most characteristic feature of faith, the believer's relationship of dialogue with God. Prayer is composed of words, and verbal communication is the most genuinely human. Prayer spontaneously adopts the form of a dialogue between human beings and God, and the most expressive sign of the bond created by faith is the dialogue form, so inseparable from genuine love.

The four traditional forms of prayer – petition, adoration, thanksgiving and expiation – can be reduced to two: petition, which includes asking for forgiveness, and praise, which includes thanksgiving. In all religions the most spontaneous and primitive form of prayer is petition, and this might lead us to suspect that petitionary prayer is not adequate to express Christian faith, which is more at home in prayer of praise and thanksgiving. But we must bear in mind that thanksgiving and petition are not in conflict, but complementary, in that they attempt to express the true relationship of human beings and God from different points of view. Moreover, they correspond to two basic attitudes of all religious feeling – wonder and fear – which in turn are linked to two fundamental aspects of human feeling: enjoyment and desire. Christian faith cannot ignore the aspects embodied in prayer of thanksgiving and in petitionary prayer, since to believe, in the last resort, means accepting life as grace and as a task, as reality and promise, as honour and responsibility.

But we always have to pay attention to the radical difference introduced by Christian faith into both types of prayer, as compared with the corresponding versions in natural religion. When, in faith, we praise and thank God, we are not purporting to give him anything, but to express our acceptance of life as his gift, free and wonderful. And when we ask him for something, we are not trying to make him act in our place and violate the autonomous system of secondary causes, but we are making ourselves more aware of our responsibilities for the transformation of the world, not as independent beings, but as totally upheld by the power of God.

Christian faith needs to give praise and to ask. It is true that Christianity insists on the importance of praise, above all in its eucharistic form, but it cannot dispense with petition – on the contrary, if it did, such essential dimensions of Christian life as the practical fight against evil and the active transformation of history would be in danger of being forgotten. What Christian faith cannot do is to accept a form of petitionary prayer linked to a concept of God which considers God simply as the Being who explains and controls, directly and immediately, the functioning of the world and history. If it did, prayer would become a means of using God, either because of a belief that God needed our prayers or because of a desire to use God's power to meet human needs. Faith goes beyond the idea of a God who can be used and the magical use of prayer, because the God of Christian faith is the foundation and ground of all being and can only be laid hold of by a free and total surrender and acceptance, and prayer is no more than the expression of the bond between individual human beings and the community and this freely available God.

However, we must not fall into the error of believing that the whole efficacy of petitionary prayer consists in its ability to make us more aware of our needs and our obligations. In reality, it is a matter not just of intellectual explanation, but also of a real practical efficacy, whether considered from the point of view of human action or from that of the grace of God.

In this respect we have to overcome a concept of petitionary prayer which does not do justice to the real relationships between human activity and divine influence; I mean one which thinks of prayer as a recourse to God *in extremis* when all human possibilities have been exhausted. This is the conception underlying remarks like, 'Humanly speaking we've done everything we can; all we can do now is pray.' Such an attitude forgets that human activity and God's grace are not mutually exclusive, nor simply juxtaposed, but fundamentally coextensive, so that when human beings act, they are always supported by the power of God. Work therefore does not remove the need for prayer nor prayer replace work, but the two dimensions interpenetrate, on the principle of the old monastic motto: *Ora et labora*.

The efficacy of prayer can be seen if we regard it as a special type of language known as 'performative', the main function of which is not to express theoretical content but to have a practical effect. Performative language produces an 'existential induction', that is, it induces in its users a particular emotional and practical disposition which places it in a particular area of reality. In prayer we use many typically performative verbs: 'ask', 'beg', 'give thanks', 'praise', 'promise'. All these verbs presuppose particular underlying attitudes: trust, veneration, submission, contrition, etc. But such attitudes are brought into play at the moment when, thanks to the uttering of the words, the appropriate action is performed. The performative verb is not a description of the attitude presupposed by its use; its purpose is not to indicate the existence of such an attitude. I would say that the attitude exists because of the utterance of the words. The language of prayer brings about what it signifies: it is not merely a language which conveys information, but a language which expresses commitment.[4]

In communication between human beings, when someone asks another person for something, he or she not only communicates a desire to the other but, for the petition to be effective, places himself or herself in an attitude which makes it possible for the desired favour to be granted. In the case of petitionary prayer and intercession, those praying, in the act of asking God for something, place themselves before him in the only existential posture appropriate for receiving from his grace the object of the petition. This attitude does not mean abdicating one's own responsibility but, on the contrary, committing oneself more deeply to the action which makes possible the achievement of the goal, since God never acts without allowing for free human collaboration.

Accordingly, prayer is always efficacious, provided it is sincere, that is, is in accord with its essential nature as performative language. Thus when, for example, in the Good Friday universal prayer, we ask that God 'may heal the sick, comfort the dying, give safety to travellers, free those unjustly deprived of liberty, and rid the world of falsehood, hunger and disease', we do not expect God to effect all these things by himself or in some miraculous way. At the same time as we ask for all these blessings, we commit ourselves to achieving them through our own free and responsible action, in the conviction that divine grace does not cancel out our actions, but presupposes and encourages them. Indeed, if we are not prepared to do on our own account what we ask God in his mercy to do, we would be better not to write prayers. We should remember the lesson Jesus gave us when he taught us the Lord's Prayer (Matt. 6.7–15): he makes it a condition of the sincerity of our prayer to God for forgiveness that we genuinely forgive others. To ask God for peace and justice and not to work for peace and justice is to falsify prayer at its root. However, to work for peace and justice without making them a constant object of prayer is to corrupt the genuine meaning of Christian action. If we cannot pray idly, equally we cannot act as Christians unless we 'keep praying in the Spirit on every possible occasion' (Eph. 6.18).

It would be wrong to think, therefore, that the efficacy of prayer depends exclusively on the psychological force of its performative role. Its efficacy is much more linked to the Lord's own promise: 'Whatever you ask for in my name I will do' (John 14.13). Accordingly, the highest degree of efficacy of petitionary prayer is achieved in the context of liturgical prayer, since its status as performative language is then enhanced by the link with the worship of the whole community, through which God's saving action in Christ is made present again. Consequently, the prayer of the faithful, which takes place in the celebration of the mass, if done well, constitutes a paradigm or constant model for any type of petitionary prayer by Christians.

III. Does habitual use of the universal prayer teach us to combine prayer and commitment?

While it is true that in the mass there are other moments of petition and intercession, there can be no doubt that petitionary prayer *par excellence* is represented primarily by the universal prayer or prayer of the faithful. There are, of course, within the eucharistic prayer or anaphora, various types of intercession, for the universal church, for the particular assembly which is celebrating, for the dead, for the celebrants. However, in addition to their intercessory dimension, all these prayers have the function of reviving the memory of all the faithful – in union with the Lord's 'memorial' and the 'commemoration' of the saints and the departed – and of thus helping to give the eucharist a family atmosphere which makes a reality of the community of the 'holy people' gathered round the altar to offer to God the 'sacrifice of praise'.

The universal prayer is the church's typical prayer of petition or intercession, and has two very important characteristics: it is a prayer made directly by the faithful, exercising their priesthood, and it is an intercession open to all the needs of the church and the world. It is a privileged moment, which can enable the participants in the celebration to acquire a clear awareness of their responsibilities towards the many needs of humankind. Now, however, I want to analyse how far the habitual use of the prayer of the faithful really achieves this.

As a liturgical prayer, the universal prayer is objectively directed towards bearing fruit in works of sanctification, that is, Christian commitment. Remember that any liturgical act, in virtue of signifying and effecting salvation, is permanently united to the three dimensions of past, present and future. Accordingly, petitionary prayer is necessarily linked with the evocation or anamnesis of facts of the past and with the proclamation or prophecy of future realities, and thus has an effect on the present. With regard to the past, liturgical prayer is a memorial of the saving work of Christ, not only, however, as a psychological recollection of past acts, but also as a reactualization of their saving power. With regard to the present, liturgical prayer is a plea for the divine power, which is able to repeat *hic et nunc* the wonders of the past, not only for the subjective sanctification of the members of the community, but also as an objective offer of salvation. With regard to the future, liturgical prayer is a provocation, in the double sense of involving the members of the church in a moral commitment for the immediate future and of nourishing their hope that salvation will be realized in the eschatological future.

There is no doubt that the habitual practice of the universal prayer – when carried out with respect for the rules governing it, which in any case are very flexible – helps to induce in Christians a number of attitudes necessary for true prayer. So, for example, the very fact that the prayer of the faithful occurs, as the Council's Constitution on the Liturgy says (53), 'after the gospel and the homily', clearly shows that it is the climax of the whole liturgy of the Word and, in a sense, the people's reply to the word of God. Thus we see that in the dialogue between God and humankind which gives rise to the prayer, the initiative comes from God himself, not human beings, reflecting the general principle of the economy of salvation: God first loved us (cf. John 4.10).

The fact that the prayer of the faithful is prescribed especially for Sundays and days of obligation and, more generally, at public masses, shows the church's concern that this prayer should be a real community prayer. This underlines an essential element of true Christian prayer: the Christian never prays alone, but always with Christ and fellow Christians, so that individual prayer is always related to the community, and community prayer sinks roots in the depths of the individual. Moreover, in the formulation of the prayer of the faithful, all the members of the assembly participate in order: the president exhorting to prayer and concluding the prayers, the deacon or other minister naming the specific intentions and the people praying actively either by common invocations or in silence and with the final Amen. This makes plain that the community which is the active subject of the prayer is really the church, that is, the 'holy people gathered and ordered under the direction of its pastors'.[5]

Many other aspects of the prayer of the faithful help to emphasize essential dimensions of true Christian prayer: the obligation to pray for the whole church and for the whole world reminds us that Christians cannot limit their concern to the narrow sphere of their individual needs – nor even those of their immediate community – but must be open to genuinely universal and ecumenical horizons. The essential mention of the mediation of Christ in the formulation of the prayer of the faithful is a constant reminder that, in Christianity, it is Christ who teaches us to pray and also prays with us, presenting our universal intercession to the Father in the power of the Holy Spirit. The variety of ways in which the people can participate in the prayer of the faithful – including silence and various physical positions (such as kneeling, traditional in the solemn prayers of Good Friday and worth reviving) – indicates that the prayer can be expressed in very different ways, and that the body plays a crucial role, since prayer is an act which involves the whole person.

In my view, the aspect which is most in danger of being neglected in the usual way of formulating the prayer of the faithful is the one I have tried to stress most in this section, the unbreakable connection between prayer and life-commitment. There are two reasons for this. The first has to do with the literary form of petitionary prayer, in which what we say when we pray is not, 'We promise to act,' but, 'Lord, act.' This makes it difficult to do as some modern writers suggest, among them J. Gevaert:

> Petitionary prayer should not be presented as a petition that God should do things instead of us. Even in the public invocations during eucharistic celebration, human responsibility should receive proper stress. We pray far too much that God should give food to the hungry, that God should restore peace, or that God should unite families. If we really want to take seriously the autonomy of the world and specific human responsibilities in these matters, we should not ask God to sort things out, and dispense human beings from their responsibilities. That would be to suggest an attitude of exaggerated passivity towards reality, and prayer would look like an alibi and an escape.[6]

The second reason for the lack of connection between prayer and commitment lies in what I mentioned earlier as a positive aspect: the obligation to pray for general needs of the whole church and the whole human race. While mentioning universal problems broadens Christians' vision and prevents them from being trapped in their own egoistic world, it may also give them a sense of impotence as they realize how difficult it is to make a personal contribution to such situations. It is, of course, no solution to this problem to fall into the error criticized by P. Tena: 'Listening to some versions of the prayer of the faithful, one feels that one is listening to a newspaper report or to veiled, but barely concealed, accusations.'[7] We have to try to find a balance between the universal and the particular in which, as J. Bellavista says, 'the weight falls on the first element – it should not be primarily a prayer for the needs of the local community or those present. Nonetheless it would be very unhelpful to those praying if there was no room in the prayer for the needs, desires, ideas, circumstances, events and varying conditions of local churches, communities and individuals.'[8]

IV. Suggestions for renewing the prayer of the faithful

I believe that the signs of weariness which can be seen in many places with regard to the use of the prayer of the faithful are due to a general failure to find an adequate way of combining petitionary prayer and the life-commitment of Christians. Some people suggest that we should change even the traditional literary form of the petitions and so, instead of crying, 'Lord, hear our prayer,' say something like, 'Lord, we promise you,' or, 'Lord, we commit ourselves.' I do not think it is necessary to make such a radical change in the traditional formulas of petitionary prayer. The important thing is that Christians should realize that they cannot pray for things without obligations, and that every sincere petition must be accompanied by genuine commitment. It is also important for it to be clearly shown that the prayer does not spring primarily from a sense of our own or others' needs, but from an attentive listening to the word of God. In short, for Christians' prayer of petition and intercession to be fully evangelical it must, being inherently an expression of hope, emerge as the fruit of faith and produce effective love.

Accordingly, I think it very useful that from time to time the two fundamental parameters of petitionary prayer – response to the word of God and stimulus to action and commitment – should be given explicit expression. This can take many forms. The link between the prayer of the faithful and the word of God which has previously been heard can be made explicit by prefacing the petitions with one or two phrases taken from the biblical readings. The relation of the universal prayer to the specific commitments of those praying can be encouraged by an attempt to mention real needs known at first hand by the members of the community, so that the whole assembly and each individual feels called on to join in doing something about them. All this requires a careful preparation of the prayer of the faithful, equal to, if not greater than, that of the homily.

A practical example of a prayer of the faithful devised to link it to the word of God can be found in the text prepared by the publication *Misa dominical* of the Pastoral Liturgy Centre of Barcelona for 29 January 1989. This was the Fourth Sunday of Ordinary Time, Cycle C, and the gospel of the mass was Luke 4.21–30.

> Let us pray to the Father that all people may obtain the full salvation which Jesus Christ proclaimed to us.
> Today, before our petitions let us recall the words of the gospel. Let us pray using the response, 'We beg you, hear us.'
> – *He won the approval of all, and they were astonished by the gracious words that came from his lips.*
> That the pastors of the church may speak, with freedom and courage about the demands of love between human beings, let us pray to the Lord.
> – *No prophet is ever accepted in his own country.*
> That fear and respect of persons may not make us hold back in our Christian commitment to God and neighbour, let us pray to the Lord.
> – *Elijah was not sent to any of the many widows in Israel, but to a widow at Zarepath in Sidon.*
> That the good news of the gospel may be proclaimed to all, especially the poor and neglected in our society, let us pray to the Lord.
> – *But Jesus passed straight through the crowd and walked away.*
> That we may keep alive the spirit of welcome for all, so that we do not lose the presence of Christ among us, let us pray to the Lord.
> Father, hear our prayers and pour out your Spirit over the church and the whole world. Through Jesus Christ . . .

The reference to the Holy Spirit which appears in the ending of this prayer of the faithful gives me an excuse for a final observation. Ultimately, what we Christians should be asking the Father for is the gift of the Spirit (cf. Luke 11.13). But to ask for the Spirit is in no sense to abdicate the responsibilities we have as human beings and Christians, since it is that Spirit of whom Jesus proclaimed: 'The Spirit of the Lord is on me, for he has anointed me to bring the good news to the afflicted. He has sent me to proclaim liberty to captives, sight to the blind, to let the oppressed go free, to proclaim a year of favour from the Lord' (Luke 4.18–19). To ask for the Spirit is, then, synonymous with working tirelessly for liberation from all oppressions, for the remedying of all injustices, for the elimination of all evils, physical and moral, in the world.

Every truly Christian petition resolves itself into an epiclesis of the Spirit and in this way acquires the certainty of always being heard, as well as becoming a support and force for Christian commitment. The Father never refuses the Holy Spirit to those who ask him for it in the name of his

Son, Jesus Christ, and the Christian who ventures to formulate a prayer for the Spirit cannot fail to be faithful to the inner promptings of that same Spirit. Thus, to ask for the Spirit is to commit oneself to love and freedom.

Translated by Francis McDonagh

Notes

1. For such an account see P. de Clerck, *La 'prière universelle' dans les liturgies latines anciennes*, Münster 1977.
2. P. Tena, 'La identidad de la oración de los fieles', *Oración de las horas*, 1976, pp. 8, 19–23.
3. On what follows, cf. my article, 'Pedir es comprometerse', *Phase* 20, 1980, 179–86.
4. Cf. J. Ladrière, 'The Performativity of Liturgical Language', *Concilium*, 1973/2, pp. 50–61.
5. Cf. Vatican II, *Constitution on the Liturgy*, no. 26.
6. J. Gevaert, 'La preghiera di domanda nella città secolarizata', in E. Ancilli (ed.), *La preghiera*, Rome 1988, Vol. I, p. 446.
7. Tena, 'La identidad de la oración' (n. 2), p. 22.
8. J. Bellavista, 'La oración de los fieles', *Phase* 28, 1988, p. 268.

The Prayer of the Roads: Forms of Prayer in Popular Latin American Catholicism

Marcelo de Barros Souza

I. A methodological invitation

I bless you, Father, Lord of heaven and earth, for hiding these things from the learned and the clever and revealing them to little children (Matt. 11.25).

In recent years, throughout Latin America, these words have resonated with a new and transforming force. They have confirmed in us Christians the conviction that our vocation is to be like the under-class, disciples of the Lord in communion with the poor of this continent, who are in their vast majority both oppressed and Christian.

If we commit ourselves to join in their journey towards liberation we are also invited to understand and accept their forms of religious expression and their forms of prayer.

On the Latin American continent, in addition to the many popular religions, Catholicism itself, among the mass of the people, took on different expressions in accordance with the origin and culture of the communities. So, for example, the popular Catholicism of the descendants of Spaniards and Portuguese has a different stucture and expresses itself differently from the Catholicism of Afro-American and indigenous groups.

Since we are on the subject of popular Catholicism, we should be aware of the differences, even if there are aspects in common to the different regions and cultural groups. Many popular prayers are part of these common elements.

In order to understand these prayers better, the best way is to try and tune in emotionally to the way the mass of the people pray. In order to achieve this, I invite you to imagine these pages as a pilgrimage to the wonderful shrine which is the faith of the poor. This will enable us to contemplate, even if only partially, the beauties produced by the poor through the inspiration of the Spirit of God. We can be certain that this will help us to recover our joy in prayer.

II. A faith in movement

In Guadelupe, Mexico, there is the sacred hill of Tepeyac, where the 'Little Black Virgin', the patroness of the continent, is venerated. In Brazil she is venerated as Aparecida, the Virgin of the Apparition. On the banks of Lake Titicaca the people of the Andes practise devotion to our Lady of Copacabana.

All over the continent, countless centres of pilgrimage draw the Catholic faithful. In general these shrines were not central for the official church, and a number were recognized only with difficulty by the hierarchy. But it was here that the people showed the strength of their faith and their way of praying.

It is true that a pilgrimage does not include the whole world of popular religion, but it does express such a wealth of aspects and manifestations of its faith and devotion that it can help us enter at least a little way into the heart of this secret shrine, the people's prayer.

For the majority of the people a pilgrimage is a fundamental form of prayer. Of course, any and every procession is fundamental. People love religious festivals, but they would not know what to make of a feast without a procession. A pilgrimage is a great procession made at least at important stages of life. To make a pilgrimage is to pray with one's feet on the road and one's whole body in movement.

Perhaps we can say that on pilgrimages the people of Latin America take up before God and his saints their position as the seventy per cent excluded from ownership of land, the vast majority of whom are obliged to live as migrants in search of work, a home and something like decent living conditions.[1]

One of the oldest prayers still said today by many agricultural workers in various parts of Brazil expresses this situation:

> O God, guide my fate
> in this land of pilgrimage.
> I am weak, but you are strong.

Do not take your hand away from me
in this hostile land.
I go about full of terror
with danger all around.
Guide my heart, O God.
Guard me from the devouring plague,
Keep temptation far from me.
Open the crystal fountains
from which the living waters flow.
Give me divine guidance, O God,
that my steps may go in the right way
with God and the Virgin Mary at my side. Amen.[2]

A pilgrimage is a festive event. It brings together, for a few days in the year, thousands and thousands of pilgrims. They organize themselves and come together, on foot, in lorries, by bus, and begin their prayers already at their point of departure. The whole journey is a prayer which culminates at the shrine and receives confirmation of God's welcome in mass and benediction.

A popular shrine has the feel of a sacred space which the people themselves have designated as a sacrament of the presence and action of God. As Bonhoeffer said, 'In my opinion it is not Christian to want to take our thoughts and feelings too quickly and too directly from the Old Testament':[3] the pilgrimage shrines on our continent combine elements of both Testaments.

The pilgrims call Juazeiro, Aparecida do Norte or Guadelupe, 'the holy city'. They make their way to this centre and take possession of this free land, the only one in which they can pitch camp, sell, buy, meet one another and have their celebrations.

Even in a simple rural chapel, during the novena of a saint the chapel forecourt becomes this sacred space of life, freedom and communion. Letting off rockets, attending mass, following the procession, taking part in the auction and later doing 'the saint's dance': all this forms part of a single act of worship.

This worship is collective, but within it each person fulfils his or her promise, and has his or her own reason for making this pilgrimage. The individual and the collective interact perfectly, just as the various fixed times, for mass, a procession or other communal acts, harmonize with times for lighting candles, kissing the saint's ribbon and making one's private devotions.

III. Prayer which grows out of life

Though many middle-class families are attached to traditional Catholicism, the force of its rites comes from the agricultural workers and the poor, especially the rural poor. Let us visit, on a sort of contemplative pilgrimage, some of the elements and features of popular prayer.

(a) The penitence of the poor

From the first centuries of Christianity pilgrimages have had a penitential character. In popular Catholicism in Latin America this spirit is still strong.

On pilgrimages we find the penitence of those who reveal themselves publicly as repentant sinners come to beg God's pardon. There are those sought by the police, prostitutes who feel themselves to be sinners, sons not blessed by their fathers, and those who feel themselves tempted by the devil. Many travel on foot and without money, wearing penitential garb and dependent on the charity of others.

On the road they are welcomed by other worshippers, and this forms part of their pilgrimage. There are shrines at which even today penitents go up steps on their knees, take part in the procession with stones on their heads and even make public confessions.

In addition to these penitents who accept this status publicly, popular pilgrimages have for everyone a strong element of conversion ('leaving one's home', 'turning to God') and of the celebration of forgiveness. For many, the sacrament of confession is an essential part of the pilgrimage. If there are few priests and a pilgrim is unable to make his or her confession, there are prayers and acts of contrition which are in one sense confession without a priest.[4]

It is true that when we see the poor insist so much on their sense of being sinners, we may suspect that an oppressive society and the traditionalist church have played a part in this. However, in addition to this fear of sin there is a discovery among the people of the greatness of God and of the love of the Father who always forgives. Certainly, this is one of the most explicitly evangelical elements of popular prayer, but one understood and practised in terms of a culture and social situation different from those the church encourages today.

(b) The promises

If you go on a pilgrimage with our poor people, what you will certainly see most is a huge number of people making offerings to fulfil promises. People do not make promises just on pilgrimages. One of the most common forms in which poor people ask God for the things they need is to make a promise to him, Our Lady or some saint.

Observing from the outside, one might think that this was a commercial transaction with God: if he gives such and such, he receives a candle or a mass or a sacrifice. This may be true in some cases, but the true sense of popular promises is much deeper. Poor people's promises are based on trust in God's fundamental promise, and they fit into the two basic forms of prayer: petition and praise.

Popular prayer in all religions and cultures seems to consist more of petition than anything else. And indeed, since the people pray out of the reality of their lives, and that reality is full of want and need, prayer expresses this in the form of requests.

In their prayers people ask for everything. They need health on a continent of entire peoples condemned to illnesses such as dengue fever, malaria, leprosy and other diseases which have been conquered in the rich countries decades ago. In Latin America the Catholic people pray to be cured of serious illnesses, and even from specks in the eye, toothache and attacks of choking. They also pray to get a house of their own, schooling for their children, or to be able to settle a debt. It is their way of connecting prayer and life.

In traditional environments these petitions are made through short formulas and rhyming couplets which are easy to memorize. Those who do not know how to read have the prayer written on a sheet of paper, which they fold and put in a purse hanging round their necks. According to the type of prayer and the need, there are rules about daily repetition or not.

Less specific petitions also take a form of prayer of which the people are very fond, litanies. There are various litanies, but the most popular is the litany of our Lady (the Litany of Loreto), which is used at the rosary and in novenas. It is a simple form of prayer, based on the repetition of short formulas without any intellectual pretensions, sometimes including terms the meaning of which has been lost. The important thing is that it fixes the heart of the person praying on God and his saints. It is certainly a form of prayer different from the Western style, but has resemblances with the prayer of Jesus and the practice of the mantra in Asia. This type of prayer, which has always been individual, here takes on a communal and even liturgical dimension.

In the most remote rural environments of Brazil there are also other types of prayer which we can understand only when we understand the lives of the people. In the last few years in Brazil alone an average of two people a week have been murdered because of land problems. Large landowners are organizing nothing short of a war against agricultural labourers who try to retain possession of a piece of land in order to survive.

Communities of rural workers involved in the church's new pastoral action no longer use the traditional prayers, but in more traditional places the workers have prayers 'for sealing the body' and others 'against enemies'. Take, for example, this, which is one of the best-known prayers in the interior of the state of Minas Gerais for protecting the body:

Our Father dear, who guides me safely here;
God is my godfather and our Lady my godmother.
He has made a cross on my head, + that by night or day the fiend may not come near.
The father blesses me + and the Son gives me light.
Great is the holy Spirit and the name of Jesus.[5]

In the typical style of Brazilian popular piety, in this type of petition, we find elements from Psalms such as 7; 10; 60; and 109, and others which ask for protection in dangerous passages in life, such as 121 (120) and even 23 (22).

As in the Psalms, the people's petition is connected to the everyday realities of rural life, the failure of the rains, the danger of storms, the fear provoked by lightning, crop diseases and so on. It is understandable that Christians educated in other social and theological environments should be surprised by this type of prayer. To understand such prayers better we have to understand the spirit with which the people say them.

They are part of popular 'devotion'. A 'devotee' is a person who has a special affection for a particular saint. He or she has a special relationship of trust (faith) and filial affection with the saint.

In Afro-Brazilian religion each person is the 'child of an Orixá'. In the Brazilian North-East there is a distinction as to whether a person is or is not a pilgrim of Juazeiro, whether he or she is an associate of *meu Padim* (literally 'my godfather'), an affectionate name used by his devotees for the saint of Juazeiro, Padre Cícero, who was canonized by the people against the wishes of the hierarchy. God is the father and Padre Cícero the godfather of the pilgrims.

It is within this personal and communal relationship (covenant!) that the people make their promises and ask for their vital necessities. They know that God is their only help. The petitions come from the heart, and do not just ask for things; they ask for God himself as gift and strength for the life of his people.

'With God I lay me down to rest. With God I get up' says one of the best-known prayers of the Brazilian Catholic people. Another prayer ends with the words: 'Be with me, Jesus, Mary and Joseph. My soul is yours.'

A well-known Brazilian popular song says:

> They asked me why I came here
> to pray on pilgrimage, prayers and peace
> in misadventure. Since I don't know how to pray,
> I just wanted to be there and look, look, look.
> [*Pilgrimage of Renato Teixeira*]

Comparison with one of the stories told about St John Vianney is irresistible. A peasant explained to him how he prayed: 'I look at him and he looks at me, and so the time goes by.'

The heart of the devotion is the love with which the worshipper honours his or her saint. Is not this 'spirit of adoption as sons and daughters' the heart of true Christian piety? In traditional theology the term 'devotion' ended up as a synonym for 'pious exercises', as opposed to liturgical worship. In popular Catholicism devotion, it is the love of God shown in the heart of believers which makes them pray and serve the Lord. The person who has had faith and made a vow recognizes that his or her vow was answered and goes on a pilgrimage to keep it.

A pilgrimage, however, is not just a prayer of petition. It is principally a movement of praise and thanks. It is the celebration of thanksgiving.

Nevertheless our people never separate petition from praise. All the people's expressions of religion are very rich in blessings, praises and tributes. At the heart of the petitions there can be heard affirmations of praise and affection for God, Jesus and the saints. The 'God save you' which begins so many popular prayers is a good parallel to the 'Alleluia' or 'Praise the Lord' of the Psalms. 'The people celebrate and sing, even from the depths of their hardship. Song and celebration are not far distant from trial. Was not a furnace in Babylon the source of the prayer of the three young men?'[6]

(c) 'The obligations'

Many people who are faithful to their morning and night prayers and never miss their patron saint's novena explain this by saying that it is 'an obligation'. The worshippers fulfil their obligation by decorating the litter on which the saint's statue is carried, lighting candles for the saint and letting off rockets on the feast-day. They rest from work and fulfil their vows. In some cases this 'obligation' may give rise to a religion of fear or coercion. More often, it is a commitment like a 'love pact', which makes the worshipper behave like a friend of the saint he or she is obliged to 'honour'.

With the change from an agricultural to an urban and industrial society, work and living conditions often prevent devotees from fulfilling their 'obligations'. The fact that, despite being oppressed, they adapt to the circumstances is a sign that they have freedom of heart.

There are obligations which are broader than a promise. Whereas a promise is made and kept occasionally, an obligation is a whole-life commitment. In some shrines, for example, it is common for pilgrims to come wearing the saint's dress. Also common on pilgrimages is the obligation to give alms and to share food with other pilgrims. This type of commitment reveals a prayer not just based on the needs of life, but also linked to a commitment of charity and sharing.

IV. When celebration and life mix

Looked at from outside, the people's prayers may sometimes seem merely external and social. Their real strength is revealed in gestures, symbols and social rituals.

There is a cultural difference between the Afro-American communities of Brazil's coasts or Esmeraldo in Ecuador or Cartagena in Colombia, and Andean peoples or indigenous groups in Amazonia. Whereas the indigenous peoples display a wisdom shown in the silence and interiority of a race which has been subjugated and undergone suffering, the descendants of Africans appear playful, talkative and constantly sociable. In both cases, however, prayer is linked to celebration. To pray is to celebrate.

In Latin America the liturgical renewal carried out in the wake of the Second Vatican Council brought a simplification of rubrics, a greater adaptation of the celebrations to modern urban situations and one great boon for all, greater access to Holy Scripture. However, it moved the official liturgy still further away from the habits of prayer of the people, who require colour, exuberant gestures and free time.

Today pastoral work with the popular classes attempts to accept the pilgrimages, blessings, processions and feasts popular with the people and to achieve a greater inculturation of the Roman liturgy. It attempts to combine in the celebration personal prayer and community expression, interiority and celebration, popular feeling and sacramental objectivity.

The people's spirituality is centred on the cross, but is able to give a festive character even to the procession of the dead Jesus on Good Friday.

The Brazilian Bishops' Conference, in its General Assembly of April 1989, published a document entitled 'The Promotion of Liturgical Life in Brazil'. In this study the bishops endorse the liturgical adaptations already carried out by pastors and welcome a sound and authentic inculturation.[7] In this eagerness the better to integrate liturgical prayer with greater use of the Bible and to accept the people's forms of prayer, a team of Brazilian liturgists has published, with the approval of the Bishops' Conference, a *Divine Office for the Communities*. The book collects ancient prayers from popular Catholicism and combines them with the custom the people have in various parts of Brazil of saying the office of the Immaculate Conception, of St Francis or of the souls. The result is not just an abbreviated version of the office, but a genuine attempt to create popular liturgical prayer which embodies the central tradition of the church, the Psalms, the Bible readings and the celebration of the liturgical year.[8]

V. Challenges and hopes

Many people regard popular Catholicism as doomed by the passage of time. And it is true that in Brazil alone 50 million people are forced to live far from their regions of origin. This process which has forced the vast majority of Latin Americans, in order to survive, to leave the country for the poor settlements on the outskirts of the cities, or to travel to other regions, is bringing about a great cultural change. Television and other mass communications are imposing the behaviour patterns of New York on Amazonian villages and peasant squatter settlements in Rio Grande do Sul. This produces a cultural gap between the older members, who resist with their symbolic universe, and the young, who yield to the charms of a world from which they are barred.

In the process, certainly, the rituals and prayers of popular Catholicism come under threat. Usually they reflect a world and an outlook which no longer exist in the cities, and not even in many rural areas.

Another challenge is the difficulty popular Catholicism presents for ecumenism. The expressions of popular Catholicism come from a time when the Catholic Church was isolated, condemned other churches and was dominated by clericalism and hierarchical triumphalism. Its language seems very different from that of the Bible; its devotions are not christocentric – on the contrary, they are directed towards the Virgin Mary and the saints. Its taste for sacred gestures and objects can sometimes seem superstition and even idolatry. In the pastoral ministry to the popular classes this difficulty has been faced. Love of the people and relativization of precise concepts in favour of the option for the poor has made possible a much greater participation by Protestants committed to the popular movement. Catholic pastoral workers are not always able to combine in the right measure appreciation of popular religion and a respectful but critical dialogue in order to attempt the building of unity.

What is beyond doubt is that the interpretation the poor are producing of the Bible, and the ever deeper discovery of the person of Jesus Christ, will help all of us to accept the soul of popular culture, to appreciate its form of prayer and at the same time to integrate it better into the transforming power of the gospel and the present-day experience of our churches. This is already occurring to some extent in meetings of base communities, biblical novenas and land pilgrimages.

VI. Final blessing

It is impossible not to be moved at the end of pilgrimages by the solemn blessing of the pilgrims with their working implements and vehicles ready for the road. Moreover, the blessing is a form of prayer which our people love deeply and which links them to the story of Abraham and the whole biblical tradition.

One song used to close celebrations in the North-East of Brazil begins like this:

> Being together with such gladness.
> Saying goodbye is sadness.

Our pilgrimage towards an understanding and contemplation of how the poor pray has only been begun and suggested in these pages. May this love unite us in solidarity with the oppressed, to defend their lives and their freedom and to express their faith with their faces and their culture.

> The earth has yielded its produce;
> God, our God, has blessed us (Psalm 67.7).

Translated by Francis McDonagh

Notes

1. M. de Barros Souza and J. L. Caravias, *Teologia da Terra*, Petropolis, RJ 1988, p. 20.
2. *Com Deus me deito, com Deus me levanto, Estudos da CNBB*, No. 17, São Paulo, p. 60.
3. *Letters and Papers from Prison*, London and New York [3]1967, p. 157.
4. *Com Deus me deito* (n. 2).
5. Ibid.
6. João Batista Salles, 'A oração ao Deus na Bíblia', *Estudos Bíblicos* 10, 1986, p. 68.
7. Conferência Nacional dos Bispos do Brasil, *Animação da vida litúrgica no Brasil*, CNBB document No. 10, São Paulo 1989, see esp. Ch. IX.
8. *Offício Divino das Comunidades*, São Paulo, 1988.

From Slave to Friend: Prayer and the Gratuitous

Isabelle Chareire

The petitionary prayer widely attested by the Gospels[1] is nowadays often ruled out because it would seem to go back to an image of God, and therefore of ourselves, that we reject. The feeling of dependence on the deity, a prominent form of nineteenth-century religious devotion,[2] has become notably suspect. Such prayer, as a resort to a magical power, a devaluation of this world and a disengagement from it, would seem to contradict a God who becomes incarnate and invites us to incarnate him there. Praise seems to us to be a more appropriate way of honouring the God of Jesus Christ. But is this not to be rather over-hasty in brushing aside the question; is that all that is at issue in the debate? Are not the qualities of petition, thanksgiving and praise[3] dependent on one another? Do we not have to rethink each of them in the light of the quality of our relationship to God? To eliminate one at the expense of the other would be no use without looking for what motivates both.

Nietzsche's denunciation of the Christian God raises a question which allows us to put our practical prayers in the melting-pot. That God is none other than the projection of our fear of living; that is why we want him to call us to account, in order to assuage the anguish which seizes us in the face of meaningless suffering.

To escape this kind of relationship, which is necessarily perverse, given such an image of the divine, we associate a God with love offered without conditions or limits. This purely gratuitous relationship to which this Other invites us will give rise to a new question: why and how are we to address this infinite divine liberality which knows in advance what we need (cf. Matt. 6.8), gives it to us, and, as the liturgy proclaims, to the glory of which our praises add nothing?

While this Love cannot cease to offer itself, we can refuse to open ourselves to it. This possibility within us introduces a flaw into our encounter with the Other: it is never realized fully by human beings. On the other hand, our identity as finite beings, beyond any dimension of sinfulness, prevents us from realizing a relationship which transcends any expression in language, the place of mediation *par excellence*. In the encounter between pure divine love and our humanity, prayer would then be the place in which our tension towards God constantly strips itself of that which attaches itself to it in order to launch out on a movement in which love is the sole justification.

I. The pitiless creditor

From joyful self-affirmation to feelings of guilt

'What is revolting about suffering is not suffering in itself but the meaninglessness of suffering,' writes F. Nietzsche in his *Genealogy of Morals*.[4] That is why Christianity[5] tried to justify this suffering. The idea of God came into being to explain this inexplicable fact. But if this suffering has become intolerable, it is as a result of a profound change in human behaviour.

Originally, man confronted the world joyfully and militantly, in a serene affirmation of himself and his vital energy. Then, the domination of a constraining political force provoked a violent break. Behind 'these terrible bulwarks'[6] the shapeless masses began to be organized. But this oppression obliged the individual to turn his instincts in on himself; this repressed freedom which can no longer expand produces a new kind of being. Outward adversity is no longer confonted spontaneously, but it disturbs the self. So while for the warrior there is no distinction between the power and the act – the force which he expresses is a natural one – a split now begins to open up in the conscience between act and will; the notion of responsibility arises out of this capacity of human beings to choose whether or not to display their force, whether or not to act. In this process, the conscience is progressively refined; everything becomes the object of deliberation and leads to a bad conscience. On the other hand, once force is channelled, relations from then on take the form of exchanges. Once the individual has become measurable under political constraint, everything becomes calculable, can be evaluated and enters into an inexorable logic of exchange.

The conjunction of these two factors leads to the birth of what Nietzsche calls negative ideals: distinterestedness, self-sacrifice, and so on. In fact, if the self has to constrain itself, its existence cannot be justified solely in terms of itself; from then on the attention paid to it is obscured, 'Everything can be paid off, everything must be paid off'.[7] Since nothing is given positively, but everything becomes involved in a system of exchange which makes everyone a creditor or a debtor, the individual is no longer certain of his or her right to live. Living is no longer a natural given, but relates to a merit to be paid. Finally a third factor appears, that of origins: the idea of debt is extended to forebears, to whom one owes one's life. This relationship to ancestral origins is soon transformed into a more basic origin, God.[8] It is from the gods, or from God, that I have life, existence and being; it is from them, from him, that I can also fear any threat.

Human beings are eternally indebted for the life which they have been given; and if this is diminished in misfortune or suffering, it is because it has not been worthy. Suffering is the price to be paid for a radical indignity. This indignity is of the moral order since, because they are responsible for their acts, human beings are always susceptible to being blameworthy. So by suffering they pay the debt of a moral duty which they have failed to perform.

The Christian – eternally a debtor

Christianity brings this feeling of guiltiness to a climax. God ransoms the sins of humanity by giving himself as a victim to his debtor: a victim whom the debtor can then bring as a perfect sacrifice before his creditor.[9]

Here we can easily recognize the theory of vicarious satisfaction from *Cur Deus homo*. Anselm of Canterbury thinks of the bond between the creature and the creator in terms of property, according to the way in which the social and economic relations of his time functioned:[10] the lord has an absolute right over the serf. In this framework sin is a matter of not rendering to God, the absolute master, what is owed to him. Satisfaction for sin then requires not only the restitution to God of what is his by right, but in addition compensation for the damage that has been done. Now the magnitude of the offence is estimated by its quality; so with regard to God the offence is infinite, and the situation of the sinner would seem desperate because he is powerless to remedy this offence. Only the God-Man, by his free acceptance of death, can satisfy this creditor.

Nietzsche denounces an utterly perverse logic in this system: from now on human beings are perpetually insolvent. If the creditor is the very one who makes good the debt, the debtor is definitively alienated from his creditor. This perfect benevolence takes away all desire for independence.

If that is the case, the prayer of the Christian to God is that of the slave to his Lord. It is a total alienation of prayer, which can only be servile imploration or doubtful flattery. In this perspective, petition is not the only form of prayer to be suspect, for what is the significance of praising the one on whom I depend for everything? We are no more than courtiers on the lookout for whatever honour or sinecure his Majesty is willing to grant us.

I should make it clear that here I am describing an extreme situation. Strictly speaking these are possible perversions, and can easily be discovered in a theology which for all that does not exclude gestures of pure gratuitousness – and does so for two reasons. On the one hand, the experience of debt and that of grace are both part of a profound structure of human nature: it seems difficult for us to envisage the absolute absence of both. In this connection it is interesting to see to what degree, in the prayers of St Anselm, the deep feeling of wretchedness never excludes an immense confidence in the love of God and a real joy.[11] The figure of the God of grace can never be completely absent from Christian experience. On the other hand, in the last resort the link between theology and Christian experience is quite complex. Except when it functions in a completely ideological way, theology never determines prayer completely: practice is never a duplication of theory. And if theology is a valuable instrument for criticizing our practices, these can subvert it in their turn. So the one can never be entirely reduced to the other.

Divine indifference?

Given this stifling benevolence described by Nietzsche, or this 'unquenchable interest' of the ancient gods, was not Epicurus right in thinking that 'if there are gods they have no concern for us',[12] and that basically:

The blessed and immortal nature knows no trouble itself nor causes trouble to any other, so that it is never constrained by anger or favour. For all such things exist only in the weak.[13]

If Epicurus describes this interest in humankind as weakness, it is because in his eyes it reveals an inadequacy: God would need this other who was capable of evoking his anger or his kindness.

This divine indifference is profoundly alien to the Christian perspective, for which 'all the hairs of our head are counted' (Matt. 10.30). Do we then have to resign ourselves to this alienating attention of a God whom we could not escape, of whom we would have an imperative need in order to live – and vice versa – and whose mercy would allow us to make better use of this dependence? Can we not rather trace a route by which the encounter would take place under other horizons? If 'final reality never comes either to fill a gap or a void or to come close to a well filled sphere',[14] creation is the work of the pure and gratuitous love of God, and the relationship between the creator and the creature is not expressed in an independence which is ignorant of the other or in a relationship solely motivated by need. But how can we envisage what is neither dependence nor indifference?

II. The God of grace

Independence and otherness

G. Morel stresses that if we want to think of relations with the Other in the form of pure gratuitousness we have to give up putting ourselves in any perspective other than the human perspective: human beings can envisage the question of God only in terms of their humanity. The Other exists in a radical otherness and freedom which the human being cannot alienate. God is to be considered outside the need that humankind can have of him in order to justify itself to itself.

Along with this independence of the Other it is also necessary to affirm the independence of the finite. This independence recognized on both sides is not a shutting-in on oneself, but on the contrary is the only possible way of opening oneself to the Other as such; if I do not *need* the Other, or the other person, I can make authentic enquiries about this other and recognize the other in his or her otherness.

In Christianity, the sorry paradox between a God who pays very close attention to humankind and the dereliction into which this humanity is cast in times of trial, the strange silence of God, can only be understood in terms of a God who in this way shows a 'disconcerting respect'. So the mutual respect for the Other and the human being is distinguished by a 'reciprocal attention characterized by the most extreme delicacy'.[15]

This movement of openness towards the Inalienable and the One who does not alienate does not instil in us the fear and fascination of religious relationships of a sacral kind.[16] This gut fascination of the finite in the face of the infinite arises from the fact that the one is defined only in terms of the other: the difference is thought of only on the basis of the identity. Now to initiate a relationship purged of all narcissistic projections, it is necessary to posit the difference as an absolute one, and not as a flaw in identity: the finite is not the incomplete infinite, and vice versa. 'God is not like us'; to be created in the image of God does not necessarily mean to be a finite infinite. The difference between God and me, wrote Angelus Silesius, is otherness.[17] It is holiness which establishes true otherness, not sacrality.

So the relationship is no longer this rivalry which characterizes the sacral relationship in which God is the one who annihilates me or whom I devour in my narcissistic projection or even with whom I drown myself in this nothingness in which all fusion issues.

It is from the recognition of this otherness and this independence that the relationship of love arises. It is a communication in which the other is recognized, not primarily for the recognition that I could expect from him but, in his movement of recognition, for himself.

Whereas human beings can close themselves to this recognition, God is unalterable openness. One cannot imagine God turning away from human beings, no matter what their attitude, for in so doing one would be introducing an ethical modality which would veil and alter the essential grace of this communication: 'the free relationship on the part of God has no other reason than itself: it is liberality.'[18] Salvation is no longer, as in the Anselmian perspective, a fair exchange (our salvation for the death of Jesus), but the exuberance of the love of God for us.[19]

God creates by love; the notion of creation does not surreptitiously introduce at this point a limit to the human independence affirmed earlier. In fact God is not the creator of freedom but only of its conditions; strictly speaking, freedom cannot be given: it only arises from the initiative of the subject. Human beings are free from their own freedom. God realizes himself in love, and love is God; as creator he simply leaves the finite world to be independent.

This generous and discreet love does not attack those whom it addresses, but raises them up. This overflowing of self, this excess, the passion of love which is desire, joy and admiration, calls forth another desire. This is the encounter of two desires which subsist at the very heart of the relationship and which have no reason for their love other than this love itself.

Praise alone?

If I am established in my independence and my freedom, it might seem that prayer can only be praise or the wonderment of love. To ask would be to deform the true countenance of this God who knows what we need (Matt. 6.8) and who does not wait to be begged to give a superabundance of life, movement and being (cf. Acts 17.28). Why ask him for our daily bread? How could we doubt that he will give us what we need? Or again, is not to ask to renounce my independence?

Nevertheless, to stop there would be to believe that the recognition is honoured in the same way by both parties, whereas human beings can cease to respond to the free love which the Other offers them. In that case the encounter is never experienced in an absolute fullness. On the other hand, human beings, marked by their finitude, are incapable of moving in the sphere of pure desire, which is always mediated by need. Desire is as it were written on their bodies as need.

Another difficulty also emerges when we read the New Testament. While in the Gospels there is a radical call to gratuitousness, there is nevertheless indubitably the idea of retribution. We can read this paradox in a striking summary in Luke 6.35: 'Love your enemies, do good and lend without expecting anything in return. Then your reward will be great, and you will be the children of the Most High, for he is good to the ungrateful and the wicked.' The gratuitousness of the love of the children of God, the image of that of the Father, will be their reward!

Finally, it has to be stressed that if, of these two aspects of God sketched out above, only the second corresponds to the true Spirit of the God of Jesus Christ, in the name of our humanity, we are never really done, in our time, with this feeling of guiltiness which shows us to be debtors. The ambiguity of the language of the gospel could well be there to indicate this difficulty.

III. From asking to gratuitousness

Need and desire

As children we have an imperative need of others; to become adult and gain one's autonomy is to pass from a relationship of need to a relationship of desire. For the infant, parents are those who satisfy its hunger; gradually they become persons existing outside the need it has of them. When parents do not accept this transition in their child from need to desire, for fear of seeing the child become a true individual, a formidable other, when they know to such a degree what their child needs that they anticipate the child, the child cannot gain its desire. Frustration or separation is the place where the subject can become aware of its need, and only the one who is aware of need can achieve the expression of his or her desire. Emma Bovary, Flaubert's character, never has the chance of living by herself; she endures the destiny of her social condition. She cannot decide on anything, and simultaneously the idleness into which she is thrown makes her become aware of herself, but as an 'abstract' subject. Everything takes place in the indeterminacy of her dreaming: never facing a specific material frustration, but suffering quite genuinely from a frustration of ideas, she cannot achieve the expression of her desire. It is confrontation with the harsh necessity of hunger, the body and work that structures the desire of the subject. It is only through the experience of solitude that I know at what point others are necessary to me, and it is because I know this necessity within myself that I come to distinguish in conviviality what is a simple response to this need from this movement which impels me towards the other because the other is who he or she is, and because I am what I am.

Thomas Aquinas writes:

> It is necessary to distinguish between perfect and imperfect love: the first being the love of another for his own sake, as the one to whom we wish good things – in this fashion one loves his friend; the second being rather the love of something not for its own sake but for its pure utilitarian value – in this way one loves what he covets.[20]

Perfect love is this disinterested tension towards the loved one, a mobilization which does not expect any gain for itself: the beloved is loved for himself or herself. What motivates the lover's movement outside himself or herself is this desire for the other from which all self-seeking is absent. Imperfect love moves us towards the other by reason of the request that I have to make to him or her; the other exists in my eyes only to satisfy my covetousness. The other is a means by which I can return to myself. The former 'seeks no reward' (I Cor. 13.5), whereas the latter is essentially motivated by it. However, being disinterested does not signify an absence of reciprocity. And there is an effective encounter only in this reciprocity, which is an abundance of good for us. One could then understand the gospel idea of retribution not as this inexorable justice – which Nietzsche suspected of being vengeance – and which would seem to introduce an ethical condition into divine love, but as the amazing manifestation of this reciprocity. The encounter between God and human beings can only take place if the latter respond to the love which is offered them – and this response is love realized in works (cf. Matt. 25). So the opposite of gratuitousness is not reciprocity, but covetousness, that centripetal force which constantly brings the subject back to himself or herself instead of launching the subject out towards others. This is beyond question that sinful dimension which attaches human beings to themselves and makes their movement towards God more burdensome.

Asking

However, beyond this failing, in the name of our finite structure we are irremediably attached to need – that is, to those vital demands by which we live and without which we could not live. How are we to think of this link between need and desire in our relationship to God?

To someone one loves one can give in advance or, out of modesty, allow the person to make his or her demand. So the other becomes aware of his or her need and then desire. Unless a person formulates this desire it exists only in the perspective of the other and no longer in the person's independent being. Quite apart from any consideration of content – which we shall be examining later – to be able to formulate a request is a proof of independence, not of dependence. In this way God allows us freely to accede to our desire, by leaving us to formulate it. The attentive listening of the other is the place where I can put my question. The person who listens allows the one to whom he or she is listening to talk. The interlocutor allows a language. Even if there is always imbalance, a gap, between the desire and its formulation, that comes about only when it is expressed. This dialogue allows a departure beyond imagination through a comparison of the request with the possibility of its effective realization, thanks to the presence of the other.

What response does the request call for in terms of content? By borrowing money from friends I put myself in a situation of dependence if it means that I am seeking to benefit from their work without making any effort; but if I use this money to look for work, the perspective becomes radically different: I am seeking cooperation so that I do not lose my freedom. Money borrowed to achieve my financial independence allows me to pass from needing my friends to desiring them. It is because God does not respond to my need by aid which would rob me of my free initiative that I become aware that what takes place between him and me is of another order. Just as in the autonomous use of my money I discover my economic limits, so, by bringing me up against the real, prayer reveals the possibility that the request will not be satisfied. And it is in this experience that I discover God beyond what I would want to ask of him for myself, in the adventure of an encounter which is in itself a joy.

From asking to meeting

Because there is a gap between the request and the reply that the other makes, the other enters into this exchange as a subject. In the act of asking there is an interpersonal relationship.[21] In petitionary prayer this cooperation by God – who expresses himself in terms of the intimate experience of each person or the particular sensitivity of each community – a relationship of pure grace is opened up. This grace is the gift of an encounter which is its own justification.

It is an adventure from which praise arises, pure nard, the product of earthly essences and yet an impalpable perfume. This verve without return is expressed in the flesh, in sorrow and joy; like the tones of Mozart in the C Minor Mass, it is extreme incarnation, the source of the clearest elevation.

The frank affirmation in the Gospels of petitionary prayer is basically very healthy, because it takes account of this basic link in human beings between need and desire. The one is rooted in the other, which it has ceaselessly to change so that this other is not transformed into covetousness.

The two figures of God sketched out here are never radically exclusive in our consciences; perhaps we always have to fight against the creditor God in order to encounter the God of grace. We have difficulty in getting rid of our guiltiness – which often veils our real sin.[22] What stops us in the course of our discovery is this suffering in the face of which the attitude of Job is the only true one. To affirm the absolute character of the gift is also to accept the inexplicability of suffering.

Thanksgiving: here is the open horizon of the request if it becomes aware, in its movements, of the utterly free love of the One who is being asked. Asking and thanking: here are two essential tensions in our relationship to God; one is on the side of our humanity, the other on the side of eschatological joy.

Notes

1. Cf. e.g. Matt. 6.5ff. par.
2. In this connection see Schleiermacher.
3. I shall use thanksgiving and praise indiscriminately, although the first usually denotes gratitude in respect of a particular situation; be this as it may, both seem to me to relate to the same dynamic.
4. F. Nietzsche, *The Genealogy of Morals*, London 1910, 210.
5. Nietzsche stresses, ibid., 82, the frequency of this concern to take account of suffering; we find it in the ancient gods.
6. Ibid., 101.
7. Ibid., 83.
8. See ibid., 108.
9. Ibid., 111.
10. *Cur Deus homo?*, 'Why God Became Man', in *A Scholastic Miscellany*, Library of Christian Classics X, London & Philadelphia 1956, 100–83.
11. *Dictionnaire de spiritualité ascétique et mystique*, Paris 1986, 2277–8.
12. Nietzsche quotes this as a saying from Epicurus, but it does not seem to appear in the surviving works and fragments: *Epicurus. The Extant Remains*, ed. Cyril Bailey, Oxford 1926. The substance of the idea is in *To Herodotus*, 77; *To Menoeceus*, 123.
13. Epicurus, 'Principal Doctrines', I, in Bailey, *Epicurus* (n. 12).

14. G. Morel, *Questions d'homme*, 2. *L'Autre*, Paris 1977, 155. At the beginning of Part II I take up the major lines of Morel's thesis. In talking of God the author likes using the term Other, which fits in with the development of his thought.

15. Morel, *L'Autre* (n. 14), 132f.

16. By sacred I understand what is considered in terms of opposition to and competition with a sphere which would be regarded as profane; by holiness I understand what is apprehended in its absolute originality or otherness.

17. Quoted by Morel, *L'Autre* (n. 14), 138.

18. Ibid., 157.

19. On this question one could refer to J. Moingt, 'La Révélation du salut dans la mort du Christ', in *Mort pour nos péchés*, Brussels 1979.

20. *Summa Theologica* 2a 2ae qu 17 a 8.

21. Cf. D. Vasse, *Le Temps du désir*, Paris 1969, especially ch. 1, 'La prière: du besoin au désir'. For prayer as the experience of the gratuitous love of God I would recall the phrase of B. Besret in 'Libération de la prière', *Un risque appelé prière*: 'The goal of prayer is not to arouse the love of God but to make us open to that love.'

22. By guiltiness I understand the feeling of debt described earlier, and which is involved in an essentially narcissistic movement of the self; by sin I understand the awareness of having wounded the other for lack of love.

Contributors

HANS SCHALLER was born in Lucerne in 1942 and entered the Society of Jesus in 1962. He studied in Munich, Lyons and Tübingen, was Director of Studies at the Germanikum in Rome and did his doctoral studies at the Gregorian Institute there. From 1977 to 1985 he was a student chaplain in Basle. Between 1985 and 1989 he was involved in founding an association for the handicapped, Arche, in Hochwald; since 1989 he has been a student chaplain in Zurich. He has written three books: *Das Bittgebet, eine theologische Skizze* (1979), *Verbirg nicht dein Angesicht vor mir* (1982) and *Wie finde ich meinen Weg* (1986).

JUAN MARTÍN VELASCO was born in Santa Cruz del Valle, Avila in 1934. He is a priest in the Madrid diocese. He studied philosophy and theology in Madrid, Louvain, Paris, and Freiburg im Breisgau. He has been Professor of Phenomenology and Philosophy of Religion in the Pontifical University of Salamanca, Madrid site, Rector of the Madrid Seminary (1977–1987), and Director of the Istituto Superior de Pastoral (1973–1976 and from 1988). Among his publications are: *Hacia una filosofía de la religión cristiana. La obra de H. Duméry*, Madrid 1970; *Introducción a la fenomenología de la religión*, Madrid ⁴1986; *Dios en la historia de las religiones*, Madrid 1985; and *Increencia y evangelización. Del diálogo al testimonio*, Santander 1988.

LAWRENCE A. HOFFMAN was ordained as a rabbi in 1969 and received his doctorate in liturgy in 1973. He serves as Professor of Liturgy at the Hebrew Union College, New York. Active in the liturgical renewal of the American Reform Movement, he has chaired its Liturgy Committee, and composed *Gates of Understanding*, a two-volume worshipper's commentary on that movement's new liturgy, as well as the historical introduction to its current Passover Haggadah. Other publications include *The Canonization of the Synagogue Service* (1979); *Beyond the Text: A Holistic Approach to Liturgy* (1987); *The Art of Public Prayer: Not for*

Clergy Only (1988). He has also edited *The Land of Israel: Jewish Perspectives* (1986).

GEORGE SOARES-PRABHU, SJ, was born in India in 1929 and joined the Society of Jesus after graduating from the University of Bombay with a degree in chemistry in 1949. He is at present Professor of New Testament Exegesis at Jnana-Deepa Vidyappeth, the Pontifical Athanaeum of Pune, and Visiting Professor for Post-Graduate Studies in Christianity at the University of Madras. He has written *The Formula Quotations in the Infancy Narrative of Matthew*, Analecta Biblica (1976), and contributed extensively to theological journals in India.

ENZO BIANCHI was born in 1943 at Castel Boglione nel Monferrato. In 1966 he went to the village of Bose a Magnano, Vercelli, and founded an ecumenical monastic community there of which he is now the head. He is a member of the *Concilium* Advisory Committee for Spirituality and the editorial committee of the journal *Parola, Spirito e Vita*. His publications include *Il corvo di Elia* (^{8}1986), *Pregare la Parola* (^{10}1987, which has been translated into several languages), *Introduzione ai Salmi* (^{4}1982), *Il radicalismo cristiano* (^{4}1985), *Vivere la morte* (1983), *Lontano da chi?* (^{3}1984) and *Il mantello di Elia* (^{2}1985).

ULRICH EIBACH was born in Burbach, Kreis Siegen, in 1942. He studied biology, Protestant theology and philosophy in Wuppertal, Heidelberg and Bonn. Between 1974 and 1980 he was Assistant in Systematic Theology at the University of Bonn, where he gained his doctorate. Since 1982 he has been a hospital chaplain to the university clinics in Bonn and representative of the Evangelische Kirche im Rheinland for further education and questions of medical ethics. His books include *Recht auf Leben – Recht auf Sterben* (1974); *Medizin und Menschenwürde* (1976, third enlarged edition 1988); *Experimentierfeld: Werdendes Leben* (1983); *Gentechnik – der Griff nach dem Leben* (1986, ^{2}1988); *Sterbehilfe – Tötung auf Verlangen?* (1988). He has also written many articles on questions of bioethics and on pastoral care in theological and medical journals and symposia.

JOAN LLOPIS was born in Barcelona, Spain, in 1932. He studied at the university of Salamanca, at the Gregorian and at the San Anselmo Liturgical Institute in Rome. His main publications include *La inútil liturgia* (1972), *Pregar en un mòn secularitzat* (1979), *Pedir es compro-meterse* (1982) and *Què és un sagrament?* (1984).

MARCELO DE BARROS SOUZA is a Benedictine monk, prior of the monastery of the Annunciation, a small monastic community living among the agricultural workers and poor of the deprived areas in the city of Goiás Velho in central Brazil. Marcelo is a specialist in working with the Bible among the poor and was one of the founders, with Carlos Mesters and others, of CEBI, the Centre of Biblical Studies. He works as theological adviser to the Pastoral Land Commission (CPT) and, with the Brazilian association of liturgists, on liturgical inculturation. His publications include *A Bíblia e a luta pela terra* (1981); *Nossos Pais nos contaram* (a new interpretation of biblical history, 1983); *Teologia da Terra* (1988); and *Cosas de la Biblia* (1989).

ISABELLE CHAREIRE was born in 1957 at Annonay, in France. A laywoman, she studied philosophy at the state university of Lyons, where she gained a master's degree for work on Hegel. Having subsequently gained an MTh at the Catholic Faculties in Lyons, she is now working on a thesis in fundamental morality.

Members of the Advisory Committee for Spirituality

Directors

Christian Duquoc OP	Lyons	France
Casiano Florestan	Madrid	Spain

Members

Frei Betto	Sao Paulo	Brazil
Enzo Bianchi	Magnano	Italy
Carlo Carozzo	Genoa	Italy
Johannes van Galen, OCarm	Aalsmeer	Netherlands
Michel de Goedt OCD	Paris	France
Gustavo Gutiérrez	Lima	Peru
Ernest Larkin, OCarm	Phoenix, AZ	USA
Jean Leclercq OSB	Clervaux	Luxembourg
Pierre de Locht	Brussels	Belgium
Edward Malatesta SJ	San Francisco, CA	USA
Maria Martinell	Barcelona	Spain
Jan Peters OCD	Geysteren	Netherlands
Samuel Rayan SJ	Delhi	India
Samuel Ruiz	Chiapas	Mexico
Jean-Claude Sagne OP	Lyons	France
Charles Schleck CSC	Rome	Italy
Theodor Schneider	Armsheim	West Germany
Pedro Trigo	Caracas	Venezuela
Fernando de Urbina	Madrid	Spain

Members of the Board of Directors

Subscribe to Concilium

We are pleased to announce that from 1990 onwards *Concilium* will be published by Trinity Press International in the United States and SCM Press in Britain.

TPI and SCM Press are one company, spanning the world; an organization which is committed to publishing the best works of ecumenical theology in single, joint-imprint editions which are available without complication all over the world.

SCM Press, which celebrated its 60th birthday in 1989, is well-known for its wide range of theological publications; it has long been publishing the works of major theologians associated with *Concilium* : Edward Schillebeeckx, Hans Küng, Gustavo Gutierrez, Jürgen Moltmann and many others. Trinity Press International is a new development, founded in 1989 but already a major force in publishing in the USA.

All existing subscriptions placed with T. & T. Clark will be fulfilled by TPI/SCM Press. US and Canadian subscribers will in future be mailed directly from the TPI organization in Philadelphia; UK and other subscribers throughout the world will be mailed from SCM Press in London.

For the best and promptest service, new subscribers should apply as follows:

US and Canadian subscribers:
Trinity Press International, 3725 Chestnut Street, Philadelphia PA 19104
Fax: 215–387–8805

UK and other subscribers:
SCM Press, 26–30 Tottenham Road, London N1 4BZ
Fax: 071–249 3776

Existing subscribers should direct any queries about their subscriptions as above.

Subscriptions rates are as follows:
United States and Canada: $59.95
United Kingdom, Europe, the rest of the world (surface): £34.95
Airmail to countries outside Europe: £44.95

Further copies of this issue and copies of most back issues of *Concilium* are available at $12.95 (US and Canada)/ £6.95 rest of the world.